also by
margaret cho

I'm the One That I Want

riverhead books

NEW YORK

margaret
cho

I
HAVE
CHOSEN
TO
STAY
AND
FIGHT

THE BERKLEY PUBLISHING GROUP
Published by the Penguin Group
Penguin Group (USA) Inc.
375 Hudson Street, New York, New York 10014, USA

Penguin Group (Canada), 90 Eglinton Avenue East, Suite 700, Toronto, Ontario M4P 2Y3, Canada (a division of Pearson Penguin Canada Inc.) • Penguin Books Ltd., 80 Strand, London WC2R 0RL, England • Penguin Ireland, 25 St. Stephen's Green, Dublin 2, Ireland (a division of Penguin Books Ltd.) • Penguin Group (Australia), 250 Camberwell Road, Camberwell, Victoria 3124, Australia (a division of Pearson Australia Group Pty. Ltd.) • Penguin Books India Pvt. Ltd., 11 Community Centre, Panchsheel Park, New Delhi—110 017, India • Penguin Group (NZ), cnr. Airborne and Rosedale Roads, Albany, Auckland 1310, New Zealand (a division of Pearson New Zealand Ltd.) • Penguin Books (South Africa) (Pty.) Ltd., 24 Sturdee Avenue, Rosebank, Johannesburg 2196, South Africa

Penguin Books Ltd., Registered Offices:
80 Strand, London WC2R 0RL, England

First Riverhead hardcover edition: October 2005
First Riverhead trade paperback edition: October 2006
Riverhead trade paperpack ISBN: 1-59448-220-9

The Library of Congress has catalogued the Riverhead hardcover edition as follows:

Cho, Margaret.
I have chosen to stay and fight / Margaret Cho.
p. cm.
ISBN 1-57322-319-0
1. American wit and humor. I. Title.
PN6165.C56   2005   2005051042
792.702'8'092—dc22

PRINTED IN THE UNITED STATES OF AMERICA

10 9 8 7 6 5 4 3 2 1

Grateful acknowledgment is made to Alex Zaphiris for the use of the photographs on pages v, 39, 40, 209, 210, 231, and 232, and to Phil Nee for the photographs on pages 1, 2, 23, 24, 91, 92, 145, 146, 179, and 180.

A small portion of this book was published in *50 Ways to Support Gay & Lesbian Equality: The Complete Guide to Supporting Family, Friends, Neighbors—or Yourself,* edited by Meredith Maran with Angela Watrous, published by Inner Ocean Publishing, Inc., 2005.

Portions of this book have been posted on margaretcho.com.

For Al

CONTENTS

WHO DO YOU THINK YOU ARE?

"haven't we heard enough from these ancient white guys?"

Who do you think you are?

I am often asked this question.

I ask myself this question whenever I sit down to try to create something out of nothing.

What emboldens me to give my opinion of what is going on? I certainly don't fit in with any of the great political thinkers of the day. My profile doesn't match up. I am not a man, nor am I white. I am not really old enough or educated enough.

What could I possibly have to say that would be of any use to anyone?

Perhaps the things that set me apart from the commentators we are used to hearing from are the things that make my opinion worthwhile.

Haven't we heard enough from those ancient white guys? There is this silent agreement that everyone everywhere has made regarding old white men. They are the bottom line, the last word, no matter what. The saying "It's not over 'til the fat lady sings" is erroneous, because women who are fat are never listened to. It's not over until the old white guy says it's over, which sounds simple—and maybe a little angry, coming from me.

I'm not so much angry as I'm trying to find my own voice in the world, to find the courage to have a voice in the first place, then to go forth and use it, which both are monumental tasks that require a lot more confidence than you'd think. Sure, we love the underdog in movies, the funny, awkward guy beaming with the right stuff if only he could get other people to listen to him. The black sheep always seems to triumph in the end. But I'm no black sheep. I'm no dark horse. I'm something never seen before, not yet happened, untested and unsure.

How will I be received?

The only way to push forward instead of wasting away in the purgatorial procrastination of worry is to just not care what the outcome is. I need to just start running downhill with my eyes shut.

There are no guarantees that I will be able to survive in this world, where the air is rare for minorities like myself. But that suits me just fine. I'm a risk taker that way. When I buy electronic equipment, I tell them to toss the receipt. I don't need it. I gamble that it won't be faulty, that I won't have to return it, just for the measly pleasure of being able to walk away from the counter without that small slip of paper. I'm such a buccaneer. I want to swing on a rope when I leave Fry's. What a high roller I am! Throwing caution to the wind has become second nature to me, and it's a good thing, because I need courage now more than ever before.

It sounds odd to talk about the incredibly high stakes of entitling yourself to a voice and an opinion, and to allow yourself to voice that opinion, but there are a lot of people who understand so deeply what I mean that we could all break down crying in a heartbeat. When you never see anyone like yourself expressing him- or herself, then it makes you think that you just aren't supposed to do that, that you have no self to express.

My parents have lived in the United States since 1964 and they have never voted. They don't feel they have a right to. They don't feel that this is their country. Even though they are citizens, they pay taxes, they watch the news and keep up with current events, they still don't feel comfortable enough with their American life to fully participate in it. When I ask them why, they simply say, "We aren't supposed to." Any attempt to argue is thwarted by a wave of dismissal, my father distractedly moving his hand across the air, as if he could brush the subject away—and so he does. I guess he doesn't want to explain, because how can you explain something as intangible as invisibility?

move on

I was hit by quite a wave of controversy when I performed at the gala event to name the winners in the "Bush in 30 Seconds" campaign. That week was fairly tumultuous for Move On, as there were two ads out of hundreds that were submitted to their contest that equated Bush with Hitler. At the event, I said, "Bush is not Hitler. He would be if he applied himself."

It sent a shock of laughter throughout the Hammerstein Ballroom, and a shock of, well, shock through the conservative media. I was deluged with hate mail from sites like Drudge Report and freerepublic.com, telling me to shut up and take my fat chink ass back to my country. That was one of the nice ones.

The amount of racism, sexism, homophobia and hatred in general that lies just beneath the surface of the American dream is astounding and serious. The names don't hurt me; I have a built up a tolerance to that. People talk about racism in terms of tolerance, like the ability to tolerate diversity, but I approach it more like drugs. I've had so much of it, it takes a lot to get me to even notice. I actually adore that kind of hate mail, because if all you have to fight me with is prejudice then I've already won the battle, and I'm eventually going to win this war. I wrote about hate mail on my Web site, and posted all that I had received, along with the names and e-mail addresses of the guilty. This sparked many of the people reading my site to lash out in my defense, and actually prompted an incredible number of the haters to recant and apologize. I even got a letter from a minister in West Virginia who'd devoted that week's sermon to the whole issue, and he apologized on behalf of his entire congregation.

they turned off the mic

I did a gig that was not my typical show. It was a corporate convention in San Diego, the kind I normally avoid, held at a major hotel. Even though there are extravagant sums of money to be made, I hate the atmosphere. However, this event was booked by a friend; it was within a reasonable distance of my home; and I was told the employees specifically requested me.

We—my sidekick, Bruce, and my husband, Al—drove in a stretch limousine to the show in San Diego. We watched *Dogville* on our way there. I love Lars Von Trier. *Dogville* is about the exploitation and persecution of women who search only for virtue and the opportunity to do good deeds (although to describe the film in terms of only one theme is to diminish the scope and power of this extremely compelling and complex story). The film strangely fit the scene we were presented with when we arrived at our destination.

We got there early, and ran around in the suite provided for us at the hotel, eating cold pizza and chocolate cake, waiting for the time we were to perform. Finally, they fetched us and brought us down through the kitchen to the banquet hall.

There were two large screens between the stage and the doors to the room, so the audience could see what was happening up close. This didn't make sense, since the room was rather small, hardly a ballroom. It had been occupied earlier by manic teenagers trying to have a prom.

It looked bad. It felt wrong. A man gave a speech that was much applauded for seemingly no reason, after which he swept past me without acknowledging my presence. Then a woman wearing a Nu-Bra, allowing her and us to enjoy the backless fashions of the moment, underneath her black rayon sheath with rhinestone spaghetti straps and a butterfly back—you know, your "night on the town" dress—started to cry onstage about her sales staff. She was overwhelmed with emotion, and had her hand on her chest, as if her heart were about to burst with affection for her employees and she was trying to push it back in, like the monster from *Alien*. We all had to cope with the lump in her throat for several minutes, especially when she had to return to the stage after leaving because she had forgotten to name names she would never forgive herself for not naming.

This rhinestone butterfly lady finally finished; then there was a parade of the staff, mostly young people of color, that work behind the scenes at hotels, parking cars, delivering room service, turning down the beds—you know, who, like, do everything. It seemed oddly demeaning to me, as a person of color myself, that the maids and bus-boys had to undergo this kind of odd celebratory lineup, but it also seemed they were very appreciated by the audience. I was glad. Everyone deserves applause.

Bruce took the stage, and I thought he did well. He was funny and got laughs, which is what he always does. Then I took the stage, after a brief, panicked attack by a nervous woman in another black rhinestone confection, likely needing a NuBra but I wasn't sure, saying something about "language." I assumed she meant for me to go ahead and speak English.

After about ten minutes, my mic was turned off, and the band, composed of Asian, African American and Latino musicians, was hurried on stage. They looked apologetic. We wish we didn't have to do this, they all said with their eyes as they launched into a rousing rendition of "Sweet Home Alabama."

Using Lynyrd Skynyrd as a way to ethnically cleanse the stage after I was unconstitutionally censored was the most offensive thing of all. I'm a huge Skynyrd fan, and I consider it unconscionable that they played me off with "Sweet Home Alabama" to excise the "anti-American" element from the stage. Skynyrd and I are on the same side. I'm proud of the South. I wish I was from the South. I have spent enough time there to know and love it well. "Sweet Home Alabama" is one of my favorite songs, and it was appalling that they offended me with the greatest American band.

I also was offended by the five identical blond women ready to leap onto the stage after I was turned off. What were they there for? It just proves once again that pussy is not supposed to speak.

It's ironic that Skynyrd was chosen to chase me out of town like a witch when I am the true American. I feel bad because the audience, although chilly, would have eventually enjoyed and loved what I had to say. I'm sad that they were not allowed the great honor to see me perform in person.

protest this

We were getting ready to play the Houston Improv, which used to be a club called Spellbinders, where I did one of my first road gigs, where I met the brother of a man who would be introduced to me two weeks later and become my first love.

We were threatened by a local conservative group that said it would picket the show unless I was taken off the bill and fired and replaced by someone else. Sorry. Now I'm more excited than ever to meet y'all. Personally, if you are going to picket a show, fine, but the fact that you are picketing my show means you are stepping up to me, which means some very bad things could possibly happen to you. Which is why we decided to show up early, to make a human barricade between the protesters and the audience coming to the show, people who had purchased the tickets months in advance, who were closing up their shops early to have time to get ready, who had hired babysitters, who had their nails done, who got highlights in their bangs, who the night before planned out a whole outfit to wear, then totally ended up changing their mind and wearing something completely different.

Protesters, please be warned. Fans of my work are not the nicest people in the world. If you're into me, you've been through it. And if you don't know what being through it means, then you just don't know me yet. The great fan base I have built up over many years in the business comes to see me with a lot of anticipation, and they have a lot invested in what I might have to say. And they can fucking fight. They will throw down in a fucking split second, and I really don't want to see any of you protesters get hurt. Queens do not play. They will fucking kill you. Lesbians know how to throw a punch that will leave a very large bruise, and they aren't opposed to kicking men right in the balls. The underrepresented, unvoiced, ignored part of our population, the great many people who make up the Cho Army, are something you are unaware of, and they're pretty much the gang not to fuck with. We are the baddest motherfuckers on the block. I don't want to see anyone get injured, emotionally or physically. I don't want to see a drag queen make you cry. Which will happen if you show up with all your picket signs and pamphlets.

Personally, I don't think you will. If you do, I want to hear what you have to say, but before you have your say, look me in the eye and tell me your name, what your mother called you when you were little, what you do for a living, if you are married, who your children are, if you are truly happy in this life and what your family is like, then, word for word, repeat the e-mails that you have written to this figurehead in cyberspace that you don't consider a human being. I also want you to hold my hands when you do it. You can say all the things that you have already told me I am—shall I remind you? Chink, dyke, hole, whore, pig fucker; telling me to go back to where I came from, even though I am an American and was born here; fat, ugly, et al.

Bruce is also available. You can call him a nigger and a faggot! Our only wish is that you do it on camera, looking deeply into our eyes, holding our hands, never losing contact with our hearts. In return, we will love you for your courage in standing up for free speech.

We come in love. We come to love. We do love you.

flags

I must eat Lebanese food several times a week, preferably at dinnertime, if I can persuade my eating companions. I adore a coarsely chopped fattoush, with crisply toasted wedges of pita tossed with the lemony radish and parsley, alongside a creamy mouhamara, walnut paste infused with pomegranate and red peppers, and an earthy shanklish to round out the lavish but healthy repast. I love the flavors and the textures, the bite and the crunch, the sweetness of the olive, the rich depth of goat's cheese. Then the inevitable and auspicious slice of baklava, flaky and honeyed, which brings to mind ancient pleasures, biblical decadence. Everything is luscious and fresh, what food should be always.

There is a place we go on occasion, a bit far from home, but all the more worth it for the distance and the increase of longing that accompanies the lengthy drive to the suburbs. The dishes there are excellent, absolutely authentic, with an on-site bakery for toothsome sweets, and big belly dance extravaganzas on the weekend. They have an extensive catering service, where you can order an entire roast lamb for any event with just twenty-four hours' notice. I love the patio, where you can sit with Middle Eastern families, women in hijabs smoking shishas, the big hookahs that the waiters fill up with water, burning charcoal and fruit-scented tobacco. The music is Egyptian pop, and you can't help but bounce your shoulders and sing along, even though the meaning of the words remains a mystery.

Just as we pull up to this place I get to go to when I beg enough, for the first time I notice two very large American flags draped across the entrance. It's a strange sight, incongruous with the modest and humble décor. The flags nearly block out the windows, they are so big. Not just one but two flags. It's as if there was a need to emphasize the Americanness of the place. "We are American," says the first flag. "No, we *really* are!" says the second. It struck me as enormously sad, somehow awkward and tragic. Had something happened that would make the flags, the statement, necessary? Had this Middle Eastern eatery become the target of misplaced anger because of the situation in the Middle East? Or were the flags put up in order to deflect racial tension, as if to brace for the worst, akin to Floridians nailing boards over their windows before the hurricane hits. Were people dumb enough to actually vent their frustration over Iraq on a restaurant in the San Gabriel Valley? I'm sure that they are, and that makes me cynical and sick. What do they think that American is, anyway? If America is for Americans, then we must remember America as being everything that lies between its borders. Nothing can be thrown out because, according to our philosophical underpinnings, nothing is exempt. America is free; America is brave. But having to remind others of your American status, fear of being connected to the enemy because of ancestral ties, the threat so prevalent that it makes you put not one but two giant flags outside is not right. It shows how deeply un-American America has become. We have allowed alarmist and racist attitudes to take us hostage, and if these impulses are not kept in check they will behead us all.

andy rooney's got to go!

Andy Rooney's got to go! Who cares about what he thinks? I have been listening to his boring-ass opinions on the stupid things that rich white folks think about because they have the luxury of basking in the glory of his whiny, creaky "Did you ever notice?" Because they are not worried about being called "fag" at school, or having the courage and strength to press charges against a rapist, or whether the rent check is going to bounce, or the INS is going to come knocking at the door, or whether you are subtly discouraged from growing up to be what you want to be, because you never saw people that look like you doing what you want to do and you don't know if you are going to be able to be the "first," or whether your lover just died of AIDS and you're not eligible to be the beneficiary on his pension plan because you were not his "spouse," even though you had been together for twenty years, and it is likely that without his support, financially and emo-tionally—damn, just without his love surrounding you, enveloping you every day—you will lose your home and possibly the custody of his daughter, or whether your stepdad is molesting you but you can't really say anything to your mom because he is supporting you and your brother and your mom and you are scared she will have to work even harder than she already does, or whether whenever you hear the words *chink, nigger, beaner, paki, sissy, bull dyke, faggot, cunt, bitch, ho, jap*—unless that word is a term of endearment for you and is called out by someone who happens to be one of you—your face burns hot with embarrassment and shame because, through no fault of your own, you happen to be you, and apparently to the person saying it something is wrong with that.

No, I never "notice," motherfucker, because I don't have time to notice. Because there is a war that is going to happen whether the people of this country want it to or not. Because I have this concern that I may somehow lose the right to choose what I can and cannot do with my body. Because even though there is all this talk about multiculturalism in the television and movie industries, I have yet to see any evidence of it. Because the young girls try to emulate the stars they see on TV, with their big ignant heads and too small, too skinny-looking bicycle body, and die in the process.

The quiet messages that affect and alter the way we view ourselves are controlled by an elite group of ignant men just like Andy Rooney, and Jerry Lewis, and all of them who need to tell the ladies to stop talking about sports and stay on the sidelines, because we are just baby-making machines trying to be sports commentators, trying to do comedy. For that, I would like to knock their heads together like coconuts.

These are the extreme examples, the obvious ones that people can get mad about—like when Jay Leno made jokes about Koreans eating dog—but the hidden messages, our invisibility, is more harmful to us than any of those fools on the "board." I loved the slogan "Silence = Death" that Act Up used for the fight against AIDS in the '80s. If we don't talk about this epidemic, we are going to die. I want to take it further. For all those aforementioned people who might not understand what I'm talking about, silence is worse than death. When we never see who we are, never hear what we think about things, what we are doing as a group or what we are doing individually, then it is as if we were never there in the first place. Silence = Nonexistence.

"Blue-collar" pundit, assaholic blowhard Bill O'Reilly = another old white man I wish I could pop the head of.

"Done went on the Atkins Diet" Rush Limbaugh = I'm glad he is deaf, because finally maybe he'll shut up and hopefully = silence.

That Motherfucker Tucker on CNN's *Crossfire,* always with his bow tie and running his mouth like he's a mug of smug root beer = my foot in his ass when I go on that show.

That is, *if* I ever get to go on that show, because whenever they ask me to be on any kind of news program to comment on something, it is always about something Asian. I know some other shit too. I have a lot of opinions about things. But that's not important to segment producers. They need me to validate them by being some sort of authority on whatever Asian thing they need help with. That justifies my reason for being there, and being allowed to have an opinion, because somehow there is this notion that since I share the same skin color as a quarter of the earth's population I've got to know everything about it. This attitude = ignant.

All I ask for is a chance to have the same kind of forum, the same right to speak, the same credibility as these (in my opinion) wrong-ass, ignant fools. But the producers of these types of shows think that I will talk only about tai chi, where to get the best sushi on the West Side, how to feng-shui your office—and then, coming up after the break, our special guest, Martin Yan! And I think he brought his cleaver. Stay tuned! *Gong!* The fact that the media at large, both liberal and conservative, look at my race before they hear my voice = fucked-up shit, I've had all that I can take, things are going to change because they just have to. Because I said so. Because we exist. Because all of us together = Power.

All I ever saw after September 11 was old white man after old white man on CNN talking about what happened. Theirs were the only opinions that seemed to count, because, when the shit hits the fan, the old white men are the only ones who can deal with it. They are the only ones who get to speak during a crisis. Like these guys are saying, "Okay, let's get serious here. We gotta take care of business." No women, no people of color, except for a precious few Muslim and Arab Americans talking about how this event has fucked them up because everybody is blaming them just because they have a similar skin color as the perpetrators of this terrible crime. All the stupid violence that was aimed at their community would be like arresting

Emmanuel Lewis when it was Gary Coleman who punched that lady, which equals blindness, fear of other cultures, misplaced rage, racism, making up our own definition of who is really "American." And, of course, do I even have to say this one more time? Ignant.

We need to wake up. It's time to start some shit. Alarm clock = Revolution.

let's roll

We are a nation divided, which is obvious. The problem is, the division is keeping a monarchy in place. We are supposed to be ruled by ourselves, but I have yet to see evidence of it in my lifetime, the turbulent teenage years of this still very adolescent country.

I can't believe Bush won, either, but there's no time to despair.

What is needed now is action, not hopelessness. What is important is the tremendous progress that has been made in mobilizing people to bring about change. Remember, more voters turned out in 2004 than at any time in the last three decades. Although it might be said that we can't expect change overnight, there really was a very rapid shift in the way we view politics. We are no longer afraid to voice our opinions, to use our power, to pool our resources, to allow our differences to unite us instead of keeping us apart.

These new ways of looking at ourselves politically redefine what it means to be an American. It took our, until now, very passive identity and turned us all into revolutionaries. In a short time, we became activists, something that lay dormant in many of us and had not been awakened until now.

The polarizing of the population has produced the wondrous gift of debate, and we are more aware and politicized than ever before. There is very little ambiguity as to which side you are on. And while conservative views may be the order of the day, that could change at any moment.

Politics used to be shrouded in mystery, and was considered the elusive territory of the elite, but this, too, is changing rapidly. Americans nowadays live with the immediacy of politics, politics directly affecting the way we live more drastically than ever. Yet the powers that be haven't quite considered the strength of our sheer numbers. We are watching politics with an educated and cynical eye, which as a generation we haven't done at all until now. With all this caution and attention focused on our "elected" officials, we have a moment where we can grasp the brass ring of self-government. In the immortal words of DMX, "They don't know, who we be." But they will, and they will be sorry.

The Bush administration will be sorry they won this battle, for they now look forward to losing the war. Ultimately, a government cannot defeat its people, no matter how much power they assume or how corrupt they are. For us, there is only opportunity. Now we have the chance to challenge everything, fight everything. The possibilities are endless. All the polls, all the posturing, all the opinions that we endured during the election provide us with a valuable education on how we think and act as a country.

There are a huge number of us on the same side. We had no idea how many of us there were before. We constitute roughly half of the nation, probably more. If we refuse to concede to apathy, then we can roll up our sleeves and get dirty.

And the Republicans don't know how much fun we can have being nasty.

Life is a tragedy for those who feel and a comedy for those who think. It is vital to mourn for the victims of this government, but not at the expense of losing our sense of humor. Our ability to laugh coincides directly with our ability to fight. If we can make fun of it, we can transcend it.

With many lives at stake in a full-blown war being fought by our kids in Iraq; with cataclysmic errors in national security causing our civil liberties to be severely crippled; with too great a divide between the haves and the have-nots, culminating in the worst economic situation in nearly eight decades; with the threat to women's rights by insane religious fanatics who seek to ban abortion and therefore do away with equality; with the aberration of freedom that is the Federal Marriage Amendment and the dehumanization of gay and lesbian Americans; attacks on Social Security . . . If we can make fun of it, we can transcend it.

Unfortunately for the Republicans, this is not an action film, and therefore having the Terminator on your side is no advantage. Might does not equal right, just as we must wake up to the hard, cold realization that the majority should not be allowed to rule simply because it is the majority. The majority is responsible for slavery, segregation, lynching, denying women and minorities the vote, Japanese internment and a million other injustices and inhumanities. Fortunately, this majority holds power by a very small margin. There are certain things the majority has no right to mess with, certain things that are definitely worth fighting for—worth defending, and worth offending.

If we just don't allow ourselves to sit back and let the only-just-barely majority rule, then we have the advantage. Everything they try to do can be shot down, because we are watching. We are everywhere, and we know that now. It's an exciting time, and I have to say I'm thrilled at the possibilities, because now what is in front of us is the big show where the Bush administration goes down, Bangkok style, on their constituency and on themselves.

So whatever warrior rituals you might have, I suggest that you do them. Whether it is carbo loading or drinking down a dozen raw eggs, putting on war paint or applying your reddest lipstick, drawing pictures of Republicans on the walls of your cave and stabbing them with your spear, dressing yourself up in animal skins and taking lots of hallucinogens, listening to AC/DC or Public Enemy or Heart cranked up so loud it distorts, come on! "BARRACUDA!!!!!"

Do whatever it takes to get your war on. We need soldiers to fight the war at home. We gotta represent our 'hood, where justice, peace, equality and freedom live.

We have a date to rumble with stupidity, ignorance, prejudice, laziness, hatred and greed. Victory is sweet, but revenge is sweeter, and we will know both sooner than we think.

I am tired of holding out for a hero. I believe that as a generation that has yet to claim this as our nation, just by being ourselves and demanding what we want we can be profoundly heroic. In those fateful words that fake American hero George W. Bush stole from real American hero Todd Beamer to justify the abominable Iraq war, "Let's roll!"

GIVE PEACE A CHANCE

"my attitude toward peace does not depend on which war we are discussing. i think that words should do the work of bombs."

**y attitude toward peace** does not depend on which war we are discussing. I think that words should do the work of bombs. Killing only begets more killing. At some point, one side has to be the bigger one, and just turn around and go home. It's surrender, but it isn't the coward's way out. And if it is, who gives a shit? I'm a coward, then. But, fuck, I'm still alive. I can still use my legs, and get the fuck out of here.

My Korean heritage doesn't sway me one bit. I'm not even sure where the Korean Peninsula is, or why there was a war there, or what side we were on or why my ancestry should have anything to do with my belief system today. I am *super* American. I've even got a flag. I sleep wrapped up in it, *The Who—The Kids Are Alright* style. I love America. I'm not moving. It's cool. I just don't like seeing dead people. I'm just like that kid in *The Sixth Sense.* I see dead people, and I don't like it.

Get this crazy shit over with. Stop the fantasy that we need to be defending freedom, because we don't even have freedom in our own country yet.

What right do we have to appoint ourselves the freedom fighters of the world? If we are so good at it, where's it at? I don't see no gay people getting married. I don't see no innocent people in jail getting released. I don't see no freedom of speech, nor do I see health care reform, let alone equal rights for anyone. All I see—that's right—is dead people, and ads for Viagra, Cialis, Levitra and Enzyte.

So many drugs for those unable to get it up, and keep it up. I am superglad about your four-hour erection, but I was wondering, where is that cure for AIDS? Yeah, AIDS. Remember that? We were kind of needing a cure, like, really, about more than twenty years ago. All this research money has been spent on keeping Bob Dole going like the Energizer Bunny. How's this helping us with the problem of entirely too many dead people, and that we are making more of them every day?

And our government, who we are bound to by the fact that we elected them, does not seem to care one bit. They are unfazed by any amount of travesty, loss, tragedy, death, destruction. They call these acts "abhorrent," but have yet to find the words to apologize. I know that Cheney is at the White House with his thesaurus, so that George W. Bush will be able to learn himself one new word a day, to describe how bad shit is, but, really, all he needs is "sorry." Why is that so hard?

Why is all this so hard? Why do these old men need it so hard?

public enemy #1

Okay, we got Saddam Hussein. Under the Styrofoam, beneath the rug, in a spider hole, and he came out looking like a crazy homeless man, or former president James Garfield, however you choose to see it. He was caught in what might well have been his grave, because he was really lying under ground, breathing through a tube, without high-speed Internet access or ranch dressing, knowing he's missing all those great holiday parties, knowing what hell must be like. I was watching the footage on the news channels over and over, and on and on, 'til the break of dawn, and they keep looking in his mouth, picking through his hair. He just looks like one of the patients in *Awakenings* who wouldn't wake up no matter what Robin Williams would do. Then there are the makeover pictures, before spider hole, after spider hole.

I'm fully aware of Saddam Hussein's evil reign, and I believe that his capture is righteous, in that there is a need for humanity to bring an enemy to justice and avenge a wrong, but where will this justice land us? What justice will serve us as Americans? Please know that the capture of this heinous murderer is something that I do agree was a long time coming, but the media fucking makes it look like President George "Dumb and Dubya" Bush went down into that dirty grave himself and dragged him out by that long, white, Rip van Winkle beard. It builds up Bush like Indiana DUMBFUCK Jones, and he's not. He didn't go out there with a bullwhip and wearing a leather bomber jacket and kick anybody's ass. Bush is no hero. He didn't do shit. Shit: he didn't do it.

It was not our right to have become the world's bully and start this war in the first place. If this war truly was intended to free the people of Iraq, then it should have been started over a quarter of a century ago. If this was about saving Iraq for the emancipation of the Iraqi people, not oil, then Saddam Hussein would be a long-forgotten name. Remember the shah, anyone?

What it boils down to is this: the conservatives removed the feather from Saddam's ass and stuck it in their own dunce cap, and where does that leave us? Capture or no capture, Bush still thinks that same-sex marriage should be illegal. Bush still thinks that we need to preach abstinence to high school students instead of telling them what to do realistically about sex. Bush still thinks that the Spanish language is called "talkin' Mexican." Bush still believes that abortion is wrong, and therefore it's not the choice of the individual woman involved. His jurisdiction includes everybody and your mama's uterus. Bush still stands by the edict that even if about ten percent of the soldiers responsible for the capture of Saddam—the real heroes, the men and women at the heart of the operation—are homosexuals (more like ninety percent if lesbians were involved), he has the nerve to uphold "Don't ask, don't tell." And you *know* there were lesbians involved. The dykes do you a mean hide-and-seek, and they don't play.

Abomination, that Bush would do this and still call himself a hero.

Bush is a liar and a thief, and uses God's name like they grew up together in the 'hood, like they got thug love. Bush still believes in the joining of church and state, which is antithetical to why this nation was born in the first place. Bush still is our own worst enemy, and now that Saddam Hussein has been captured and photographed in his big baggy underwear, that shoots Bush up the charts to Public Enemy #1.

the war on errorism

George W. Bush was once again talking about how the war in Iraq is worthwhile because, basically, we're there. Of course, we're there because of weapons of mass destruction that do not exist. And Bush is still using billions of taxpayer dollars to build himself a platform from which to say, "You know I'm right. I'm right. I'm so right. I am! I am!!!!!"

This is just another stoopid bid for attention that is digging Bush into an even bigger hole, and proving once again that he is innately, genetically incapable of admitting that he's the idiot that he is. Of course, there's the possibility that he has no idea how dumb he is, in which case we're fucked.

Unbeknownst to us, we've been sent on a suicide mission, like landing a manned rocket on the surface of the sun. He's leading a fight against terrorism, when, really, we're fighting errorism. This fool has fingered the wrong countries, the wrong people, the wrong everyone and everything, and in so doing has risked the lives of thousands of American children. Don't you think the soldiers look like they came straight from their high school yearbooks, too young to be over in Iraq, fighting for no reason?

Bush has been so wrong-headed in every decision he has made in the Oval Office that it should be called the "Obtuse Office" because he be so dumb the room changed shape. The walls buckle further with each statement he makes, as if to try to squeeze him out of the seat of commander in chief.

The famous ghosts who haunt the White House gather in the Red Room to gossip about him night after night. Mary Todd Lincoln keeps opening up the windows, hoping that Dubya will just fall out one of them, which scares me, actually, because then Dick Cheney would be in charge, and which would you rather have, Dumb or Evil? I guess I would go with Dumb, but, you know, it's just revisiting that same old question, "Is the presidential office half full or half empty?" Dolley Madison's high-pitched wails in the White House's dark corridors are intended to upset his slumber, but, of course Dubya doesn't notice. He just snores, sawing logs all night long, because, you know, he's so stupid he probably suffers from sleep apnea and breathes with his mouth open. And JFK walks the ceilings, pacing back and forth, wondering whether the nation will ever be returned to itself.

Is it a democracy anymore? Is there hope anymore? Is there even fucking going to be an America the Beautiful after this reign of error? Are we talking prequel, sequel or epilogue? It seems like only one thing to me: a eulogy.

indignant, ignant rumsfeld

Whenever I watch Rumsfeld's live press conferences on CNN, it's really, really scary. He totally discarded the prison abuse scandal, and eviscerated the press for focusing on it, as if the stories weren't true and the media was making a big deal out of nothing, and, in doing so, worsening the situation in Iraq. He goes on about how because of our takeover of Afghanistan, women there are now able to vote where before they couldn't. They can even wear "gray" shoes. What? Like he's wearing a THIS IS WHAT A FEMINIST LOOKS LIKE T-shirt under his suit.

He consistently and completely glosses over the issue at hand. His technique is "indignant and ignant," and he employs it with a lot of flair. Rumsfeld takes the podium like he is already put out by people daring to have him explain his actions, then he expounds on his indignity, and then he says he doesn't know. He makes a lot of quotable indignation faux pas about how there were no high-ranking officers involved in endangering the lives of prisoners, and makes a mad owl face that says, "Give a hoot! Don't pollute!" Then he just exits the room of hotly simmering journalists to percolate with unanswered questions about the 9/11 tapes, brushing them off with a wave of his hand like they don't have the right to ask him about that, like they're pesky flies or something.

When do we get to ask those questions? Is there going to have to be another investigation? Yet another panel, or series of panels, to identify once again what went wrong? It's depressing. Hope dries up in this first summer heat and evaporates along with good grooming and patience. Everybody's hair is frizzy or flat, and we have no idea what our nation is doing in our name. I don't want to be anyone's captor, anyone's torturer.

It's unacceptable to me, both as an American and as a human being. I wish I could be ignantly indignant, but I actually care too much about life. When I see people, I know that they are for real, that they are people, that there's somebody behind those eyes, that they are dads and grads, and moms and sisters—and scapegoats—both Iraqi and American, military and civilian, and they feel just like I would feel. It sounds simple and yet it's incredibly complex. Like that R.E.M. song "Everybody Hurts." The fact is poignant, and especially difficult to bear if you believe it in your heart, when you survey all the crimes committed in our name in the War on Terror.

As Americans, to what extent are we accountable for these detestable acts? I don't know. I feel one hundred percent responsible, even though there's nothing I could do to prevent it. What good is my guilt if it's not felt by those supposedly in charge? How do I spread my guilt around so that it will negatively affect those who are truly guilty, and threaten their sanity instead of mine?

I'm being followed by an air marshal, air marshal, air marshal.

I still can't believe that Cat Stevens was taken off a flight to the U.S. and sent back overseas because he is on a "watch list." What did he do? He's Cat Stevens!!!

Okay, he's Yusuf Islam. But still, he's always and forever the Cat in my book.

Who doesn't love *Tea for the Tillerman*? What treacherous act of terrorism is he so capable of? Did the FBI log on to his Web site and see him beheading Christopher Cross? Was he declaring a holy war on all the hits of the '70s, '80s and '90s? This is just lunacy, pure and simple.

The facts remain hazy. The discovery of Cat Stevens/Yusuf Islam on the watch list prompted officials to emergency-land the plane to let the legendary singer/songwriter off. He was not detained, as far as I know, and was sent back to London. Was it because he's a prominent Muslim, and the government is trying to send a message to Islam that Muslims are not welcome here? Doesn't that violate the Constitution?

It was a heavy, emotional week, with the horrible, tragic deaths of the two American hostages at the hands of extremists, and American confidence in our security is waning. Although I'm infuriated by the war in Iraq, the incredibly barbaric and grisly killings of the two men fills me with murderous rage against the perpetrators. Of course, America is responsible for the total body count. We started it, we own it, we sow, we reap, but we are also disconnected from the responsibility of our own dirty acts of war. We don't see what we've done.

The militants post their vengeance on Web sites, and seek publicity for their displays of inhumanity. They want us to feel the loss of life as keenly as possible. It may be difficult to comprehend, but their violent exhibitionism points to the fact that they *do* value life. They knew the lives of the hostages were precious to the world. If not, then why would the world be watching, in outrage and grief?

How many American lives have been lost in this brutal and needless war? How many Iraqi? How many names do we know on either side?

It still makes me sick to see the last moments of the hostages' hideous ordeal, and I am blind with anger toward all the "zealous sons." I look at their ringleader, Zarqawi, and I think about how he's younger than me. He was in the fourth grade when I was starting high school. I humanize him because his actions are incomprehensibly inhuman. Is he any more a villain than the American soldier who picks off dozens of Iraqis with his assault rifle, or tortures prisoners at Abu Ghraib? We justify those atrocities because, well, they're doing their best for their country, but, then again, that is exactly what the hooded executioners of Tawid and Jihad are doing. The slayings of the hostages were gruesome and horrific, but what is also terrible and sad is it feeds the unquenchable thirst for American-style revenge. We see the beheadings and we think,"Kill 'em all! Let God sort it out!" It becomes a grudge match, but without the spandex and mullets.

I want to scream and shout, "Stop! We are all human beings! Stop!!! We are all people!!!," but I don't think anybody will hear it. Or that anybody will care, anyway.

What does any of this have to do with Cat Stevens? Give him back his acoustic guitar, and his freedom. Just let him ride that peace train.

good-bye

Think of all the people you love. Think about how hard it would be to never see them again. Maybe think just about one person. What if you didn't get to say good-bye? What if you didn't get to tell him or her the most important thing, something that you had meant to tell them but kept putting it off, procrastinating, then forgetting, and then you suddenly found out that you would never be able to do it because he or she was gone, forever. You'd lost this person you loved, forever. How would you feel?

What if what you had to say was, "I love you"? What if this was your lover, boyfriend, girlfriend, husband, wife? You would never hold them again, never again feel them next to you, be secure in the love you have. You would never think about the future, plan what you both would do the next time you have time to take a vacation together, wonder if the Yucatán or the Amazon is a romantic or scary adventure, because you share a fear of certain insects and tree frogs. Or if Paris is just too expensive. You wouldn't wonder if waterparks are too cold in the fall and you'd have to wait until summer. There would be no more summers together, because the time has been snatched away from you.

You will never make love, laugh, fight, eat, go to the movies, kiss, smile, dance, sing, run, skate, play the piano, swim, buy candy for, argue jokingly, tell stories, look longingly at, jump on the bed with, pet the dogs with your faces, sing along with the song in the car and get the words wrong, share a secret, gossip, cop a feel, go hear a band you both love, share a really good meal, carpool with people you don't like and make fun of them secretly later, cry, comfort, scratch backs, insist on pizza, catch them staring at you, put your arms around them, stay up too late, lean against warm bodies, feel safe with their feet sliding next to yours in bed, raise your children, go to boring dinner parties and get too drunk to drive home so you sleep in the car, spend alternate holidays with each other's families, have uncontrollable lust with, followed by mind-blowing fuck sessions lasting for hours and hours at a time, take a bath so hot one of you has to get out, all naked and wet and red and dizzy but not embarrassed because this is who you love and rarely are you shy with them, watch a TV show you both hate because the remote control is broken—merely happily, and maybe sometimes unhappily, share your life, and be with them, but you can't, because they're dead. Suddenly, unjustly, untimely, irretrievably—unconscionably dead.

As of today, one thousand eight hundred and fifty-eight U.S. soldiers dead. They could be you; they could be me. They are unavoidably us. We lose more of us every day. This list grows with each minute, each hour, each day. Look at their names, their hometowns, how young they are. Think about the heartache, the sadness, the sleepless nights because now the bed feels so very cold. Stop and really think about the war, the ludicrous, needless loss of life, the apathy of the government, the fact that Bush has yet to attend a single funeral for one of these fallen heroes, the political nightmare of these power-hungry despots using this tragedy to ratchet their careers up a notch, the nonstop talking heads on the news, the pre-9/11 investigations, the truths they've withheld, the lies we've been told.

Most of all think about each and every one of these brave men and women, some of them mere teenagers, whose first ventures out of their parents' homes and into their own lives result in their deaths. As you read their names, imagine who they loved, who loved them, and how those left behind cope now without them. Think about how we will cope without them. They're never coming home. Never. They bring back bodies, hidden beneath flags, pictures of which the government doesn't want us to see, but it's not them, anyway. They are gone, far away from this world, to heaven, I suppose, and, for their sake, I hope there is one, because here on earth it's fucking hell.

"in the darkest reaches of my imagination, it occurs to me that we are the heirs to the aftermath. we are the scavenger minority, picking at the carcass of civil rights, trying to get our measly share, so very far removed from the idea of fair . . ."

In the darkest reaches of my imagination, it occurs to me that we are the heirs to the aftermath. We are the scavenger minority, picking at the carcass of civil rights, trying to get our measly share, so very far removed from the idea of fair, but what do you expect? Being the bottom-feeders of a multicultural fish tank, we get pushed to the back of the bus by more vocal minorities that have been there and don't want to return.

I don't know how to find our voice. It catches in my throat whenever I try to use it. If I do manage to get something out, it's met with very vocal opposition from all kinds of surprising sources. When I first started, a lot of conservative Koreans would look at me and say, "She bring shame upon us." Like I wore a blazing scarlet dress to their bleached white cotillion. Whenever I speak, I know I have to be responsible because I am speaking not only for myself but for all Asian Americans, and the weight of that responsibility is too much to bear. I am too proud of my embarrassing nature. I feel like an ambassador addressing the public with four feet of wadded-up toilet paper trailing out the back of my pants.

Whenever I get hate mail, the verbal assault is always racial. People are surprised at the depth of resentment there is against Asian Americans, but it never shocks me. We are the object of hatred not only for the things we do but just for being who we are, ching-chong chinamen. Racism is one of the biggest taboos in our culture, yet most discrimination against Asian Americans goes largely unnoticed, and if it is picked up by an Asian media watch group or similar organization it's blown off by the rest of the media as a joke, as in, "Look at them. They get all up in arms over nothing."

I care less about specific incidents than I do about the general disregard. The dismissal of our anger as a racial minority is worse than any slur or epithet because it undermines our ability to react to it. I would love to be a nice, happy, model minority and say that race isn't important, racism doesn't exist, but I would be lying.

white

I would love to be white.

Not forever, but perhaps for the weekend. Don't you ever get sick of being a minority? I mean, there's the whole pride thing that a white person doesn't get to have, because you can be anything and proud but you can't be white and proud because then you seem like you're a member of the Ku Klux Klan. Having a collective heritage that is oppressed and depressing can be a lovely way to spend time after dinner on the front porch as the sun goes down. Friendships can be forged on a legacy of loathing, and how wonderful some of those bonds can be. But sometimes, I just really get sick of fighting all the time.

I am fighting when I'm sleeping. In my dreams, I must slay the dragon of European heterosexual male society, then I wake up in the morning and must be an activist. I have to watch the news and movies about the people who I am not, then translate my struggle in order to make it palatable for those people who don't have to march but are sympathetic to my voice. This is a major part of my audience, an easy ear to bend—yet I still must bend that ear myself. I make the effort and that makes the difference, and that is what I'd like a break from. What if I didn't have to bend anyone's ear? What if the playing field really was level? I'd love to see how far I could go. What if all I had to show off were my mad skills? Wouldn't I really be able to fly then?

I have posed this question to other minority artists, and get stumped by answers like, "No, not ever have I ever wanted to be white." And I just don't buy it. Why wouldn't you want things to be easier? What if you were just you, and everything you did were taken at face value, without having to consider any minority sliding scale or affirmative action factors?

i got this part . . .

I don't need any more people calling me up, saying, "I have this script that you're gonna love. There's this part for an ASIAN WOMAN—it's really not the lead, but it's such great part. Call me." The first thing that I do when I get a call like that is to press 3 for "Delete," because there's no way this part is gonna be anything good.

I have never had any desire to play a maid, a liquor store owner kicking a black person out of my store, a rude and harried waitress, a worldly-wise acupuncturist, an early-rising, loose black cotton pants–wearing elderly woman practicing tai chi in the park, a mani-curist, a prostitute, a student in an English as a Second Language course, a purveyor of exotic mushrooms and ginseng, an exchange student, a newscaster covering gang warfare in Chinatown, a woman drowning my newborn baby in a bowl, a daughter crying with my mom over our constant battle between East and West yet finally com-ing together over a particularly intense game of mah-jongg, a queen sitting on her throne in the Forbidden City being served a bowl of turtle soup by a eunuch, a peasant carrying a yoke on my shoulders like a yak trudging up Gold Mountain delivering precious water to my village, a young girl being raped and killed by GIs in the Killing Fields, a woman balancing a basket of any kind on my head, being the second wife and committing suicide to avenge the first wife by coming back as a ghost and scaring the shit out of everyone, or, alternately, committing suicide because my white lover did not come back to Japan after the war, or having him come back for me and fooling him successfully for years and years into thinking I am a woman when really I'm a dude, as if my race castrates me so much that this deception is completely feasible, or a girl, barely out of grammar school, playing violin for the president in a long, black velvet dress, or a mother, out of nowhere, screaming and then sullenly freezing out my children in an effort to terrorize them into getting better grades in school, especially in math and science, through emotional blackmail and coercion, or a teenager, figure-skating in the Olympics and winning the Gold but never getting a major endorsement contract because even though I fucking won that goddamn medal for America I will never be considered the hero that I truly am because, no matter what anybody says, this is still a racist country, or a woman giving birth to the Dalai Lama, or holding my breath for over three minutes while diving for pearls, or arguing with Elaine from *Seinfeld* about her dry cleaning, or saying, "Welcome to Japan, Mr. Bond," or being a hired assassin and flinging a ninja star, or sword-fighting up a tree, or writing my Geisha memoirs because playing weird musical instruments and powdering my neck is so fucking memorable I need to write a book about it, which actually wasn't even me writing, just some old white guy who wanted to turn my life of exploitation and prostitution into some "*Pretty Woman* During the Heien Period" fantasy, or brushing up on those concubine skills, or going anywhere with a chicken under my arm, or traveling all the way around the world to meet my birth mother for the very first time, or eating dog for lunch, or being mail-ordered for marriage to some way-out-of-my-league computer geek I have never met, or getting shot down and then rolled over by a tank in Tiananmen Square, or walking on some Jim Belushi–looking dude's back, or balancing with five other family members on a bicycle, or being knee-deep and pointy-hatted in a rice paddy, or graduating magna cum laude from Stanford, or wearing a lab coat and goggles and holding that beaker a safe distance from my body with tongs, or cooking with a wok after speedily cutting all my vegetables vertically, or binding my feet because that's what all the girls are doing this year, or wearing my long, silky black hair on one side of my head and a big flower on the other side, or doing a dance that requires me to jump over a sword, or getting off a tour bus and taking numerous photographs, or bowing, banging a gong or getting it on, or considering Pearl Harbor some kind of triumph for "my people," or making the best of being in an internment camp by starting a theater company and staging a production of *Anne Frank,* or taking all my white friends out to a Benihana and ordering for all of them, making sure nothing is too spicy, because they all think I know what to get, or dramatically escaping from Red China with none other than Richard Gere, or arranging flowers or pruning a bonsai tree, or being a "teenager" in pink lipstick and a HELLO KITTY T-shirt and miniskirt, or acting like I am five years old and pressing my knees together while making a big *O* shape with my mouth in a display of cuteness that is really just another expression of the denial of my strength as a woman, which we all know is another way I keep myself from my own power, remaining a safe and ineffectual sexual stereotype, pleasing to the status quo (see the third *Austin Powers,* the characters Fook Mi and Fook Yu), or breaking boards with my forehead, or being a prisoner of war or a spy of any kind, but obviously not a very good one or my character would be played by a white man, or explaining the mysteries of the Far East to Richard Chamberlain or to Chris Tucker—or to anyone, for that matter—because the Far East is just as much a mystery to me as it is to them, or letting anybody say, "What do I know . . . I'm just a ROUND EYES!," because that statement is condescending to me and yet so true, in that, yes, you don't know shit, and don't act like acknowledging your own ignorance excuses it, and nobody cares if you can "tell us apart" because we are not doughnuts that you need to first identify to decide if you want to eat us or not.

There is no reason to tell us apart because I don't wish to be classified, as if that makes me more human to you, or makes me more identifiable to you, as if you can understand me better, as if the country my parents came from has affected my life so much that it makes me an exotic and rare bird.

In short, don't call me about your script. I know it's going to be one of those parts, and I don't have time to be reminded once again that my story is never going to be told by anyone but me. All these characters are not who I am. They don't speak for me. They don't speak for all Asian Americans. Perhaps they speak for some, but I don't give a shit. If you have a story, tell it. But don't expect me to tell it for you. What you think I am is not who I am. What you think I want to be is so wrong I want to pop your head. If you have a script that lets me come over to your office and pop your head, then we can talk.

asian jokes?

During a recent question-and-answer session at a university, a bright, enthusiastic Asian American student asked, "The political stuff was great, but what about the Asian jokes?" This question was met with a gleeful response from the audience, and I had no real solid reply. It kind of took me aback, because the only answer I could come up with was, me being an Asian American goes without saying, and therefore, by the nature of who I am, everything I do is Asian American. I am my own perspective, and that's all. I assume that my ethnic identity is not separate from my words or my message. Perhaps that's taking too much for granted, society accepting minority opinions. I'm not sure.

I hope that people see me as having a right to debate issues that are not exclusive to Asian Americans without casting me as a "banana": yellow on the outside, white on the inside. When listening to Peter Jennings, did we think that he was actively avoiding his Canadian roots? Is Jay Leno ever held up as a spokesperson for his own ethnicity, which I actually don't know? Why don't I know? Because I have never heard him talk about it. I assume that he is European, since he's white, and therefore kind of socially "neutral," deftly able to comment on and make fun of the culture as a whole by virtue of his own socially sanctioned neutrality.

Because I am not white, am I not qualified to comment on the state of American politics? Can I not engage in hands-on activism for hot-button issues like same-sex marriage and the death penalty? I'm not trying to be hostile, but the operative word here is *trying*. We live in trying times, and as a compassionate person, with a fierce warrior spirit and a true desire to change the world, I find that there are many causes that I wish to fight for, and many enemies I wish to conquer, for to right wrongs is my true mission in life. Is my race a factor in determining whether my war cry will be heard?

As an Asian American, I have felt the effects of racism firsthand, and therefore civil rights is vitally important to me, not wanting to have my experiences repeated in generations to come. I take what I have learned from the great leaders of the civil rights movement, as well as assorted historical figures, suffragettes, religious icons, philosophers, artists and pop stars. I want to combine my knowledge with my own suffering, piecing together a kind of quilt so that we all might benefit from the warmth of understanding. My heroes are not exclusively Asian, or Asian American, but come from everywhere, as far back as recorded history allows us to see.

The people I choose to admire are not necessarily popular, not necessarily terribly well known, but they each have something to offer me, a lesson, a cautionary tale, an idea, an inspiration. I remember them much like I hope that someone in the future remembers me, that this message in a bottle will help, which I'd say is quite the ambition. This is how I would like to be remembered. Perhaps then I will transcend this ethnic face that I was born with, and my words will be as powerful as I wish them to be, but, frankly, I'd rather have that right now, while I'm still here.

I am admittedly insecure about my racial identity, an attitude that has much improved since my younger days when I absolutely abhorred it. Any attention paid to me being different was incredibly shameful for me because the wide and varied world, the melting pot of American life that I saw from the '70s, still didn't include me. If even this Big Blue Marble/"I'd like to buy the world a Coke" planet didn't acknowledge my existence, did I in fact exist at all? Dreaming of being a performer on top of that didn't help. I first was a dancer, but the mirrors became too much. Every time I would check my alignment, what a disappointing reality check! When I was dancing, there was no difference between the music and me. The beat has no race, the air has no divide. In motion, there was nothing to be; there was only movement. Then I would look up to see where I was in the dance, and I would stare back at myself, and my Asian eyes would betray my freedom and clip my wings, or, rather, I would realize that I did not have wings but Asian eyes instead. I could not see myself dancing because such an image did not exist before. I could see myself studying, slaving in a sweatshop, serving tea to businessmen, but never doing grand jetés across the studio's polished wooden floor.

I stopped dancing, and only recently took it up again after some thirty years of self-imposed retirement. I simply do not see the mirror any longer, and I do not rely on the example of someone who came before me as a kind of mental permission slip.

bamboozled

I had avoided, averted, excused myself from, promised rain checks, and procrastinated as long as I possibly could, before seeing *Bamboozled*. This brilliant Spike Lee film stars lots of heroes, friends, acquaintances and my very favorite actor/artist/activist/educator/ healer/shaman, Danny Hoch, in a hilarious Tommy Hilfigerish street-fashion magnate cameo, as well as many other wonderful performers who I've admired for years. The film is tailor-made for me, despite its tragic, melancholic yet melodic ending, but the rest of it I know first-hand from when I was developing my own television sitcom some years ago and entering into the secret race war fought in this country day in and day out. I have used my experience to fuel my own "come-back," and whole new way of working as an artist, using political and social comment to inform and educate, as opposed to following tele-vision executives around, being so certain of their rightness, possibly because of their "whiteness," although not all the players in my game were white, at least not ethnically speaking. *Bamboozled* is about a sit-com being produced by a frustrated "suit," played by Damon Wayans, the best of all the Wayans family in the way he works. He's magical. His genius is being able to play all sides of the comedic spectrum, and when he "wears" a character he completely becomes that character. Emotional changes for him come as easily as twisting a kaleidoscope, and they are just as vibrantly unexpected, just as in life, yet something that is near impossible to capture on film.

Wayans puts together the ultimate racist minstrel show, presumably for the new millennium, with old stereotypes of black America, once banned following protests so many years ago, only to be replaced by new stereotypes brought to you courtesy of the music industry in the guise of corporate hip-hop. Not that all of that shit is bad. I love it myself, but I can see how the politics of rap get thrown over easily when the stereotype is familiar, easy to dance to and unlikely to change the status quo. The show depicted in *Bamboozled* stars Savion Glover and Tommy Davidson, who go from squatting in the ghetto to lofts overlooking midtown Manhattan following their television debut. They remind me of myself at that age, when I got suckered into the Hollywood system. When you're young and hungry and nobody's ever really accepted you because of your color and class, the hurt of your own family having cast you out in the first place still inside you somewhere, you dance hard because there is no other way to live, and when opportunity knocks it's more of an abduction than a housecall.

There was one thing that I was certain of, that blaze of exceptional talent, what Savion Glover has, not to say that I have the limitless, fiery body and ability that he does, an innate understanding of what it means to dance that transcends movement to become pure beat and heart and soul, closer to lovemaking than a dance step, but I have something inside me that is rare, that has kept me alive and whole and given meaning to my life. Just as the two characters in the film were taken by showbiz charlatans in one fell swoop, so was I.

Swept up in the grand illusion that I might be able to eat, have a roof over my head, own some pretty dresses and realize, in a vastly heady way, that I could make a living doing my art, which was the only dream I had ever had, what could I say but, "Yes, where do I sign?" *Bamboozled* differs from my story because the show becomes an outrageous hit, while my show languished in relative obscurity before its innocuous death after just one season. We have in common the tremendous backlash from the communities that claimed us as their special representatives, then branded us traitors to the cause of equality and an insult to the civil rights movement, especially our own races' struggles. How hated I was, and as the *Bamboozled* duo fielded the onslaught of high-level politicos like Al Sharpton (who always is the best person to have in your movie) leading protests, blaming them outright for denigrating their race, I remembered newspaper articles reaming my parents' friends when they couldn't access my mother, trying to trace my race traitor roots from those school pictures from the '70s—you remember, happy in the foreground, pensive you superimposed behind, looking like your own ghost haunting you, or that the happy you is the presentable, public you, the pensive you is the backstabber of ethnic identity menacingly coming of age.

Never did I consider myself an Uncle Tom before being called one by numerous Asian, mostly Korean, activists who told the network that they had their protest signs ready at the first infraction of any rule they themselves had made up about what was appropriate for the race and what was not. I wasn't sure then which I hated more, my skin color or my talent. Why did they coexist in this one body of mine? What the fuck kind of shit is that? I asked for neither and got both, in great abundance, and for that I am now grateful, but it wasn't so easy back then. When is it a compliment when someone says, "No matter what EVERYBODY says, I still think you're PRETTY good?"

I took the compliment, and the paychecks, and silently faded into the background when the network decided to give up on their pet "ethnic" project, which was just too much to deal with, what with the virulent op-ed pieces, the protests, the L.A. riots still so fresh in everyone's mind, and North Korea as unpredictable then as it is now. It was apparent that Asian Americans were not to be televised. Maybe here and there, like a nice bonsai tree or bamboo fountain, but, please, not an entire television series. TOOO MUCH!!!!! Like wasabi, we are good in small doses, but too much and people think they'll go up in flames. Mind you, this is still the case, and my ex–television family hasn't been on the air in over a decade. It's doubtful that you'll see *All American Girl* on DVD, unlike *My So-Called Life,* which had the exact same life span and launched its season on the same network at the same time that we did, because we were not considered something to be nostalgic about. Just like Japanese internment, it's better to let such things slide. I think there have been some shows on recently that involved martial arts, employing more than one or two Asian American actors, but I'm not really sure what happened to those shows. I lost my numchucks ages ago, and I'm glad, because I was forever hitting my own head with them.

I can't be claimed as a hundred percent American, even though by all rights I am. I was born here, I live here, I make my money here, I spend my money here, I pay my taxes here, I make my art for American audiences, yet my ethnicity precedes me everywhere I go. I'm always the "Korean comedian." My introduction, unless I or my posse somehow manage to intervene, always includes that disclaimer, as if to say that my achievements thus far are miraculously novel, since I can speak English so darn good without any trace of an accent and I don't bow all the time or nothing.

All I know is, inside me I have the seriousness and the maturity to say, without hubris or bravado, that I am the best at what I do, which is the plain and simple truth, undisputed by most people, argued over only by those who have never seen me and/or plainly can't stand to see a woman, especially a foreign one, take that much pride and such a vaingloriously unapologetic stance in the traditional American folk art of stand-up comedy. This is not a realm I was born to nor welcomed into, yet I forced my chinky bound foot in the door, and somehow kept it open by being so fucking good. How dare I? Watch me.

So to say Asians are all over the place, making bank at the box office, kicking cinematic ass. Over here, they are still fucking kicking.

No one ever called me to tell me my show was cancelled. At least in *Bamboozled,* there is a heroic and startlingly magical implosion in the final act, which illuminates the much hidden past but in the process produces grief, and sweet hope for the future, as far as the

Asian American impact on the entertainment industry. I'm still standing—writing, working, growing AND independent, albeit reclusive,
and insanely dressed. Sometimes Asian American kids come up to me
(when they can find me) and say that they grew up watching me on
TV, and that that made them feel like they were okay. That they felt
like they were Americans, too. I like hearing that very much, and it's
enough for now.

A big thank-you, Spike Lee. You are a tremendous, important
filmmaker. You are not only a treasure of the cinematic art but
uniquely illuminating on how we view race in our culture—the real
way, not some made-up, safe, stupid *Imitation of Life* way. You never
pull any punches in a world where everyone needs to get slapped.
Please feel free to throw me a right hook anytime.

imagine

Imagine being Anna May Wong at the premiere of your film *The
Thief of Bagdad* (a title all too apropos to our times), as a Chinese
American at Grauman's Chinese Theatre, then in its Chinarama
phase, chockablock with faux orientalism, a chinkee apocalypse in
plastic and red paper. And you, surrounded by an extraction of your
own culture, are not allowed to put your hands and feet in the wet
cement to commemorate your contribution. So piquant that you actually own all the imagery surrounding you, or you did at one time but it

was taken from you to adorn this theater, to make it magical, mystical even. Remember, you are a star of the film. People lined up for blocks just to catch a glimpse of you. But your hand- and footprints will not be here permanently for the future to see that you were part of the golden age of Hollywood, even though they borrowed the golden hues of your skin without asking. This honor was reserved for the white actors. You may be desired by all the white men up there on-screen with you, and by the ones leering at you from their empress red velvet seats in the dark, but you can't marry one because it's against the law. Imagine.

Anna May Wong left Hollywood in 1927 and sailed for Europe, where she made many films and had many fans. Following in the lively dance hall footsteps of Josephine Baker, she fed the Continent's wild taste for the exotic. Germany was host to a cultural renaissance, where the Weimar Republic was in full decadent swing. They absolutely went insane for anything that was different or unique. Anna May Wong was happy there, as she felt more acceptable there. She was quoted as saying that Europe had "acceptance for people of color," and I believe that is one of the first times that phrase had ever been used. In fact, the opposite was true. Intolerance and racism were so rampant, even flagrant. IMAGINE.

I admire the savvy and complete self-confidence of Josephine Baker, whose talent and charisma are iconic and revered. Anna May Wong came home for good after her brief tour of duty, but Baker stayed on, largely in Paris, after several disastrous attempts to return to the U.S. and establish a career—completely unacceptable during the age of segregation. She got bad reviews just for being black! After being refused service at the Stork Club, she began a very open, public fight with prosegregationist columnist Walter Winchell, which the times and *The Times* dictated she could not win. She went back to the city that had put her name in lights, and she remained a tremendous star all over Europe for the rest of her life. Upon her death, in 1975, the French declared a national day of mourning, honoring her with a twenty-one-gun salute, the first American woman to be buried in France with military honors. Twenty thousand mourners turned out to grieve her passing, and the funeral blocked the streets. The NAACP subsequently designated May 20 as Josephine Baker Day.

Even though Anna May Wong has no official day, I adore her. And I like to think that I look a bit like her. I do, but not in the same way people say Asians "all look alike." We have the same kind of head, like, you know, when you see people around and you realize they have the same shape dome you do, and you kind of either love them or hate them right off the bat, depending on the relationship you have with yourself. I did a reading of a play, a biographical melodrama, which was absolutely true to life in being somewhat underplayed emotionally, for intense feelings are generally kept to oneself in most Asian cultures. I was the star, or at least I read the part of the star. The playwright was a friend of mine, Elizabeth Wong, one of the writers of the ill-fated *All American Girl*. She had written this play just for me, and hoped to garner attention for the work by putting together a group of actors and giving a reading at a building right across the street from the Ahmanson Theater in Los Angeles, not so far from Hill Street, in Chinatown, where the real Anna May Wong had grown up.

One of the actors, David Dukes, was a beautiful man in his fifties. He's one of those guys that you see in movies or on TV forever; you never know their names but you expect to see them. Your eye always makes room for actors like him, because you know his face, his motivation; because he is incredibly familiar and that familiarity is comforting. This is an everyday kind of acceptance that we have for white heterosexual male archetypes. They have every reason to be there; they populate the world, and the world exists solely for them. No, they are not to blame individually for this imbalance, but that's the real truth of the matter. It's one of those things that we, as non-white, non-heterosexual, non-male archetypes, accept, and we've been accepting it since antiquity. No big deal.

Anyway, David Dukes played my lover in the play. In between scenes, we talked about his chinchilla farm, which he was very proud of, and the production of *Bent* he had been in. I marveled at the fact that though he was not particularly famous, I knew every plane and surface on his face from memory, most recently from the ambitious Marilyn Monroe biopic with Mira Sorvino and Ashley Judd, the one playing Marilyn, the other playing Norma Jean. The best part about this film is when Marilyn is joined by Norma Jean on the therapist's couch, and they cry together as only a Gemini can. David played Arthur Miller, and he was too handsome for the part, but of course he made a fine made-for-the-screen Miller. David died unexpectedly soon after this reading.

What is strange to me is that in biopics, they always cast someone finer looking than the original, as if the reality of life must be tidied up for the camera's gaze. Nowhere is this more poignant and outrageous than in Anna May Wong's own life. She knew that there was a good film brewing in the Hollywood Hell's Kitchen. Pearl S. Buck's *The Good Earth* had been optioned, and there was a huge part—the indisputable lead, in fact—for a sympathetic Asian character. It was for O-Lan, a mother, who was sacred and not profane. This was far better by miles than the *Daughter of the Dragon* parts Wong had grown so used to. Though when she played such characters, she would always rise above them, so that you cheered for her even as she poisoned everyone. Her evil-ese was mind altering, so much so that she became good.

The historical accounts differ on the real feelings Anna May Wong had about this role. Some say that she knew she wouldn't get it, that there was no way that the Hollywood she knew so well would possibly accept her, the most famous and talented Asian American star, as the real-deal O-Lan, the most endearing Asian portrayal in Western literature to date. Others tell a different story, that she rallied and begged for the part, even arriving one day at the studio in a rickshaw dressed up as O-Lan—like Sean Young's Catwoman stunt, or Madonna's plea for Alan Parker in her video "Take a Bow" to cast her as Evita Perón. Our play centered around this particular time in Anna May Wong's life. In the third act, it is revealed that the truth is somewhere in between. Wong had hoped against hope that she could land the part, but she knew that it wasn't possible because she was, in fact, really Asian.

The part of O-Lan went to GERMAN actress Luise Rainer, who went on to win an Oscar for such an amazing job of acting under all that makeup (not unlike Charlize Theron in the recent, magnificent *Monster*). It was the final nail in the coffin for Anna May Wong's ill-timed, ill-fated career. For the rest of her life—or, rather, her Hollywood life—she would bitterly discuss this injustice with all the people around her (not many, by her own choice) before dying alone and angry in 1961.

Imagine. Knowing that you were unable to play a part because you were the right race at the wrong time. When Paul Muni was cast as the male lead, that's when the hope died. She knew that since the male and female leads were to be lovers—in fact, married—there wasn't a chance in Hollywood hell that she would win the role. Miscegenation was a misdemeanor, perhaps even a felony, punishable to the full extent of the law. Yellowface was not. Yellowface was the safe route. Yellowface was the politically correct answer. Imagine.

Even the illustrious cinematographer James Wong Howe was taken out of the running when the crew was being assembled, even though he had experience shooting all over the world, and was perfect for the job—BEHIND the camera. Imagine.

Any assumptions about how things are so much better today, how we should thank our joy luck club stars that we are no longer living in that world, seems a bit ironic. When we read the play, retelling this story of insane racism that was considered acceptable—in fact, morally responsible—behavior at the time, against the backdrop of my own television nightmare, when particularly shortsighted Korean activists were taking me to task for not hiring Korean writers or Korean actors to play the parts of my Korean family. They boycotted the show, wrote articles, mobilized en masse. We had Asian American actors, really fine ones, in all the roles, and Asian American writers in the writers' room, but the fact that they were not Korean, and that we were charged with Yellowface for this and other reasons, got the show taken off the air. IMAGINE.

The play never did get produced, although it's a spectacular work, and now it might get some attention. Anna May Wong lives on in the minds of fans and scholars of cinema's odd transition between the silent era and the talkies. She is not well respected by Asian American activist-academics, if they know of her at all, because she falls into that Charlie Chan category, a period of Asian American complicity that is, for some, best forgotten. However, she is a gay icon, worshipped by drag queens for her icily androgynous beauty and her tragedy.

John Lennon would never have written that song without Yoko Ono. Imagine.

in defense of michelle malkin

Michelle Malkin, the author of the controversial book *In Defense of Internment,* spoke at the University of California at Berkeley, fiercely trying to defend her position against the loud and angry demonstration outside protesting her appearance. Malkin's views are incredibly unpopular, especially on such a liberal campus. Her take on the racial politics of the internment of Japanese Americans during World War II is quite outrageous, especially coming from an Asian American. Just because she has a white name doesn't make her white.

Malkin is living proof that bigotry has gone multicultural. She claims that the comparison of internment to the racial profiling of Arabs and Arab Americans is unfair and a foolhardy tool of the left, who are gambling with the safety of all Americans in order to be politically correct. Advocating racism to secure our borders is part of life during war, and Malkin is here to remind us again and again how we are at war.

She ponders why affirmative action is perceived as a good thing and scrutinizing the Arab names on airline passenger lists is a bad thing. She is infuriated that the left keep on playing the internment card, seriously compromising homeland security with its insistence on those pesky civil rights.

Malkin tried speaking louder into the microphone to drown out the chants of the protesters. The American flag taped to the wall behind her fell down, which got a smattering of ironic applause among the confused and scared-looking audience. I don't blame them for being scared. I was scared for her. The protesters kept breaking into the hall, interrupting Malkin's train of thought. But she hunkered down, and kept on going, tough and diligent. She's a lot like me, I think, an "Anti-Cho." The protesters chant "SHAME!!!SHAME!!! SHAME!!!," but she refuses to be shamed by their taunts.

I feel kind of proud that the politics of race have progressed to the point where a young Asian American woman doesn't have to live within the constraints of a minority identity, which presumes a liberal bias just by virtue of the fact that if you are oppressed by the majority you would want to work against it. Malkin's position is kind of genius, actually, a new way to look at our role in American politics. We don't have to assume the mantle of the distressed minority anymore. We can be as prejudiced as whites!

Race really doesn't matter. Michelle Malkin is a revelation and revolution both. It's fairly obvious that she is being courted by conservatives, fussed over and groomed as the all-new Manchurian Candidate. She fits their need to diversify like an orthopedic shoe. It's a match made in GOP hell, an unholy union that works to everyone's advantage. The right wing gets a brand-new bag, a Skipper for Ann Coulter's Barbie. Not only that, Malkin's Asian, so that liberals will have a harder time calling her a racist even though she holds completely racist views. Malkin gets a lot of publicity and talk time for her book, which generates sales on both the right and the left. The right buys it to support their own; the left will buy it to see what all the screaming is about. And, boy, there's lots of screaming. Not since Salman Rushdie's *The Satanic Verses* have people been so pissed off at an author. I would love to issue a fatwa against her, but I'm not sure how to go about it.

The protests are counterproductive, because the right wing loves it when the left gets angry. The off-camera shouting makes us look like savages, and that's exactly the image they love to show again and again. Malkin bravely tords onward. She seems like an intelligent and interesting young woman, albeit a misguided one, and I feel protective toward her. I hope the right treats her well, and doesn't throw her away once the fury has died down. Perhaps she'll write a follow-up book, about how the Holocaust didn't happen.

Malkin's story reminds me of Errol Morris's documentary *Mr. Death*. Mr. Death, Fred A. Leuchter Jr., is a nerdy electric chair specialist who boasted an expertise on all things related to execution. He is hired by a white supremacist organization to go to Germany and disprove the existence of concentration camps. Mr. Death had never had any attention paid to him in his life. He was this dorky academic who had spent most of his life under the radar. Suddenly, he's thrust into the spotlight. Never mind it's the glare of hateful, racist, ridiculous white supremacists, the accolades are no less seductive. Here's a tragic tale of a man deprived of recognition to the point where he will attempt to revise history just to get some kind of acknowledgment. Mr. Death becomes the ultimate Holocaust revisionist. He serves the white supremacist agenda by backing up their hokey theory, and he gains redemption for his years as a "who cares?" nobody. Who could blame Malkin for wanting to follow in those footsteps?

The terrible thing about invisibility is the lengths we will go to be seen. If spouting racist propaganda and being a tool of conservatives are worth the right to live in the monochromatic world of right-wing political pandering, then I applaud Malkin's effort. She inflames the need to uphold the ideals of equality and fairness, and she puts a new face on hate. I'd be happy to argue with someone who looks a bit like me for a change.

African Americans have Clarence Thomas and Condoleezza Rice. There's a new race traitor on the block, and her name's Michelle Malkin!

why i'm political

Why am I political? Because society's consistent and constant disregard and lack of respect for minorities, even the title "minority"—when in many areas of the country, in fact, we are the majority—is too much to bear silently. Their insistence at our invisibility, whether it is as subtle as noninclusion, or as loud and violent as hate crimes, is contagious, and can make me hide from myself.

I see evidence of my own racist brainwashing when exploring the landscape of current foreign policy. I have not been able to make myself think or talk about the situation in North Korea. My avoidance stems from fear that my Americanness, hard won and fought for on a daily basis, might somehow be diminished because of my ethnic association with the perceived "enemy." My family is Korean, and we are defensive about our allegiances. There is great suspicion expressed when referring to North Koreans, as if we must distance ourselves from them as much as possible so as not to disrupt democracy.

Going out of my way to prove that I am an American does not support the idea of being American. I shouldn't have to be less interested in what might happen between North Korea and the U.S. in order to reestablish the image that I have cultivated for myself as a patriot. Also, I want to refute the assumption that being Korean might lend me any particular expertise when expounding on the political climate there. I stamp my feet and claim ignorance like a child, because it's the color of my skin that says I'm supposed to know. Trying to cut my ties with North Korea doesn't reinforce stereotypes that I currently do my best to fight; rather, it fosters new ones. I become the "one who refuses to see the self." I add to the culture of invisibility by becoming complicit with it.

I am diminished by not seeming to notice that North Korea is there, even though my family is from there, even though many of my family still live there, even though my ancestors were literally torn apart there by civil war that split the people while the people were still one. My association is so painfully close that avoidance is the only way I know to retain my American identity. It's ridiculous and embarrassing. I hate feeling this way, because it forces me to see how deeply racism has affected me. It has gotten into the way that I think, the way I live, the way I feel about myself, the way that I fear that I'm being perceived. Not only that, it's gone completely unnoticed, until I step outside myself and acknowledge the truth. I'm a racist, but it's gone underground and become distorted and returned to me utterly unrecognizable.

Prejudice and bigotry rot me from within, and the strains of these viruses are hearty and hard to kill. When I was younger, I would rudely ignore the bright-eyed Asian American kids who would stand in the courtyard and hand out sunny yellow flyers advertising after-school meetings for the new Asian Student Union. It bothered me that the flyer paper was so undeniably yellow, and that they would single me out in the crowd to give me one, as if the yellowness of my skin was a secret homing device for them. It felt like they were targeting me, because, if anyone needed it, I did. I could have used Asian unity more than the other Asian kids who rushed through the same courtyard with me. I think they sensed that, and tried harder to push the flyer into my hand. Fortunately, my racist tendencies did not keep me from having great relationships with other Asian kids in my class. We just didn't have a "union." There was no need to speak of politics, or any desire to change the status quo. If we did, it was entirely unintentional, and just part of the daily ritual of being a teen.

My insistence at being apolitical, as if that were possible, didn't end when I was young, when it could be blamed on youthful ignorance. About a decade ago, I was asked to appear on a comedy special that featured political comedians. I declined, quite plainly stating that I was not a political comedian and therefore didn't belong in the lineup. I was replaced, and I was relieved. But I look back now and think how wrong I was in my own self-assessment. Even though I lack deft impressions of befuddled politicians in my routine, that doesn't make me an apolitical entertainer. My very presence as an Asian American woman talking about race and sexuality is a political statement. I had always regarded the world of political humor as the exclusive domain of white men and immediately disqualified myself from participation. I know better now, and it's immensely pleasing when I'm referred to as a political comedian because it rings true. It feels right. It feels strong.

However, I belie my own strength when I act like North Korea isn't there, that it doesn't affect me, that I'm exempt from having to comment on it. The problem is, the conflict with North Korea unearths an unbearable conflict within myself. It brings to the forefront my own self-hatred, supported by a lifetime of suppression by the world in which I live. Self-hatred is a devastatingly difficult habit to break, especially when we are mostly unaware of it.

I try every day to challenge myself further, and I believe by doing this I slay the monster bit by bit. This is why being political is an essential part of my life. In the end, it's all I have.

emmett till and matthew shepard

In 1955, Emmett Till was a fourteen-year-old black boy living in Chicago. He was on his way to visit relatives in Money, Mississippi. He came home without himself, just his dead body, mutilated beyond belief. Emmett Till was a baby, just a boy, fucking FOURTEEN!!! He wasn't a civil rights activist. He wasn't a criminal. He didn't come to Mississippi to file complaints against the Jim Crow laws. He was visiting his great-uncle, Mose Wright. At first, he was having fun; his cousins and he became friends quickly, and they were playfully teasing one another outside of Bryant's grocery store in the middle of town. Emmett was showing off a photo he had of himself with his girlfriend, a pretty white girl. His cousins were shocked, and didn't believe him, as things were so different there in Money than in Chicago. This was the kind of town where a few weeks earlier a young black girl had been beaten almost to death for "crowding" a white woman.

Another pretty white girl, Carolyn Bryant, wife of the grocery store owner, walked by and went into a store. Emmett's cousins, knowing he would never do it, dared him to flirt with her. Little Emmett Till had been raised in the North and had no way of knowing that taking this little dare, harmless and sweet, would cost him his life. His cousins were shocked when Emmett followed the girl into the store. They tried to stop him but didn't get to. There was not much interaction between Emmett and the girl. Speculation ranges from a possible catcall, a whistle, maybe a "Bye, bye, baby." Less than two days later, Emmett Till was no longer Emmett Till. He was a broken symbol instead of how hate lives, and kills, and rots us from the inside out.

Racism is a cancer that is unstoppable if left unchecked. Emmett Till is a messianic figure because his murderers were actually tried for murder, not that it was the first time white-on-black violence had reached the courthouses in Mississippi, even with the long-standing immunity accorded white lynchers in places like Money (fucking ponder *that* for a second: immunity, LONG-STANDING), but the brutality of the Till killing, Till's age, juxtaposed with the unbearably tiny offense of flirting—fucking FLIRTING??!!!—brought so much publicity to the case that it triggered a wave of outrage across the nation. *Jet* magazine printed photographs of poor Emmett's body. Thousands attended his funeral. His mother insisted on an open casket, so that all could see what had been done to her baby.

The men charged with the murder, Roy Bryant and J. W. Milam, were declared not guilty, but in my world memory is a jail from which you can never escape, and they suffered, their cages not iron but the indelible blood and guilt, the bars and shackles from which you never will be set free.

So began the civil rights movement. Some months later, Rosa Parks refused to give up her seat on a bus, claiming her right to exist, to be equal and free, just like any other American.

We have come some distance in the continuing struggle for racial balance. But any progress rates only as fair, average, a little better than okay. There are still lynchings. And while we don't use ropes anymore, there are more efficient ways of doing it. I'm not just talking about Rodney King, but we can start there. There is worse.

Amadou Diallo, just a few years ago, shot forty-four times by four policemen in New York City for merely holding his hands up in surrender. Wouldn't you say that's lynching? Lynching. I believe that is what happened to Kobe Bryant. It seems that William Kennedy Smith can be acquitted, exonerated, welcomed back into the fold. Arnold Schwarzenegger, accused of sexually molesting sixteen-plus women, and never brought to trial, is governor of California.

Vincent Chin, a twenty-seven-year-old Chinese American, out on the town with his friends at his own bachelor party, was beaten to death by two white men. They were autoworkers, frustrated at being laid off, blaming the Japanese automobile boom. This was their chance of getting even. Who cares if Vincent Chin was an American? Who cares if Vincent Chin was not in the auto industry? Who cares if Vincent Chin was not Japanese? These men walked away with a paltry three-thousand-dollar fine. They never received a jail sentence. But they will pay, as they will never forget their own inhumanity when gripping the baseball bat that would crush Vincent's skull. They will never sleep easy again, hearing the sound of Vincent dying by their own hand. They will suffer for eternity, as God is just.

Matthew Shepard was the same as Emmett Till and Vincent Chin, the only difference being that Matthew was killed because he was gay, not because he was black or Asian. Little Matthew, hung up like a scarecrow, but also hung up like Christ, left in a Wyoming cornfield, dying as he looked up at the stars, wondering when God would come to get him.

Are you angry? I am. I'm angry, and I'm sad. I can only say that we don't have the luxury of our own privatized civil rights movements because the crimes—the ignorance, the rage, the hate against the who/what/why of some of us, is a much much larger foe. We cannot fight alone, since this battle will be lost without allies. Together, we are more than the sum of our parts. In union, in communion, in joining hands, we conquer all, because we have love on our side. Because we have God on our side. And, most important, because we have ourselves on our side.

hate crime trivial pursuit

As soon as you start to research historic cases that were clearly motivated by hatred, you realize what an obscenely deep subject you're dealing with. James Byrd Jr.'s horrible death by dragging behind a truck in Jasper, Texas, was one such crime I looked back on. It's a sad story, making me sick at the violence of it, the senselessness of it all. The man who was convicted of this murder, Lawrence Brewer, is having a hard time on death row because there are so many black people there who want to tear him limb from limb.

I would like to tear him limb from limb myself, frankly, because his crime is incredibly, unbelievably inhumane, and the punishment for it seems to merit the loss of my own humanity. Brewer was even renounced by the Imperial Wizard of the Ku Klux Klan, who was living in the town right next to Jasper at the time of Byrd's murder. The *Klan* renounced him. You have to be pretty shitty if the fucking KLAN says they don't want to have anything to do with you.

Brewer maintains his innocence, which is certainly possible. However, he sports numerous tattoos celebrating Aryan power. He even has a large image of a black man hanging from a tree emblazoned on his arm. You can bet he doesn't ever go to the showers without a number of guards flanking him. I feel sorry for him, that hate should have consumed him so much that it isn't enough having an emblem of hate emblazoned permanently on his flesh, he had to act out that stupid shit on his arm like it was the story of his life. Like it was fucking directions telling him what to do. What an asshole. And who the fuck would agree to do such a tattoo in the first place?

Tattooing is an ancient warrior art, with a kind of infernal beauty that few understand, and fewer take as seriously as they should. What self-respecting tattoo artist would say, "Oh, okay. Lynching. Gotcha!" Maybe I have no idea of the array of Aryan tattoos readily available. Maybe Brewer's tattoo of the hanging man is one you can point to on the wall, right next to MOM or the anchor or the playing cards. Man's ruin.

The fact is, our nation bringing slaves here from Africa was the biggest hate crime of all. Then, when the slaves were freed, there wasn't anywhere for them to go. Then came the reign of terror begun by the Ku Klux Klan that never really ended. And then there's the fact that none of this stuff is taught in American History, at least not in detail. It's skimmed over, to get from the Revolutionary War to landing on the moon as quickly as possible .

Then there are the laws against homosexuality. Then there's the Asian exclusion act. Then there's the internment of Japanese Americans. I'm not even going to talk about Guantánamo. And then there is the first American hate crime: taking this land from the Native Americans.

We can keep it up forever. Hate Crime Trivial Pursuit. There are more than enough hate crimes to play a decent round. I'd hoped to play it with Cornel West, bell hooks, Harvey Milk, Martin Luther King Jr. or even just a cool gang of ACLU lawyers.

I just want to love everyone. I don't care if that sounds stupid. I want to love everyone.

dear richard pryor

Dear Mr. Pryor,

We share the same birthday week. We get name-checked together on E!—it happens at the same time, along with Woody Allen and Walt Disney, but I like you the best. What can I say to thank you? How can you put laughter and salvation and the transcendental power to forget race, even for just a moment, the truth of the human condition made hilarious because of its fearlessness, the eternal power of your voice and the gratitude that I have for all you gave me and the world—in a box? Is there one big enough? I need a big-ass bow on it and shit. Not one you stick on, but actually get a ribbon and tie on, with your finger in it making the bow old-school correct.

How can this girl send you a gift that is worthy of my love for you? Because my love is big. There is nothing that I can think of in the material world valuable enough that would represent the size of this love. So here it is.

LOVE.

From, Margaret

I will hang on to the receipt in case you want to exchange it for something else. I don't know, you might prefer D. L. Hughley's love, or Gene Wilder's love. I am just leaving you some options. I wouldn't be offended in the least.

Mr. Pryor, I met you one time at this big benefit for some shit. The Hollywood players love the benefit even though we are not sure to whose benefit they be for, but they do benefit those that need publicity, so there we are. You took my hand and you looked me in the eye. We said nothing, and that moment was everything. Paul McCartney kissed me that night too, told me I was a pretty girl, and I was elated, but I forgot about him when I saw you. I remember running to get to you, and then I was before you, my knees shaking, and hands sweating, thinking of how if you hadn't done what you had done, the work you gave the world, the man you are—I wouldn't exist, not in the way I do now, not in the way I wanted to, needed to. I might not even have lived. Thank you for my life, along with all the other things I am trying to thank you for.

I saw your movies. The first one, *Live on the Sunset Strip,* changed my life, my destiny. It was the first time I realized who I was, and what I would be. I never really knew what I wanted to be when I grew up because I never saw anyone that made me want to grow up, and then there was you. You were telling your tales, making motherfuckers helpless with laughter in the aisles. Black people, white people, everyone, right at the time when we all had a hard time sitting together, we came to see you, because you were beyond race, you disarmed us, we couldn't hang on to our guns because we were trying not to pee from laughing.

Historically, you were the bridge between the civil rights movement and the America that wanted finally to be itself. The stories you told were the ones that united the Black Panther and the "honky," the feminists and the pimps, the playas and the fools, the us and the them. There was no more race war/battle of the sexes when you took the stage, there was just you, sweating like Muhammad Ali, because you were a fighter, but also a lover too, as you stopped our fighting, and started us on the idea that we could love each other. Because we laughed at the same things, we realized we had a lot more in common with each other than we thought. I count you among the others that brought change to the world that so badly needed it, Martin Luther King Jr., Malcolm X, Gloria Steinem, Rosa Parks—fuck it—Gandhi. You the man, Mr. Pryor. As important as any founding motherfucking father, any "Give me liberty or give me death" fool. You should have money with your face on it. It should be a big-ass bill, too. Like the $1,000,000,000,000 bill should have you on the front. Even that wouldn't be enough.

Thank you for the truth you told, the bravery that you had, the big balls and the brains to make the ways you almost took yourself out, killed yourself, fucking funny as fuck. How did you make the fact that you were dying from freebasing, even set yourself on fire, burning like a KKK cross running down the street—funny?!!!!!

The poet you are, the genius you are, the beauty you are—is worthy of shock and awe. You gave birth to the kind of comedy that is real, that is life, that loves the listener, loves the laugher, that has no bullshit, no front. You had the courage to be vulnerable, which nobody had, certainly not stand-up comics—maybe the dude that sang "If you're going to San Francisco/Be sure to wear flowers in your hair," whoever the fuck he was. He was vulnerable, but who gives a shit?

You were talking about the things that hurt you in life, your lovers, your past, your addictions that were taking you away from yourself, big Jim Brown who helped you and loved you and made us all wish we were Jim Brown because you held him in such high regard and you made his voice and character so full of heart and help, your monkey that the dog ate, and the dog that was sorry about it, who would stop chasing you for that day, just to mourn the loss with you, and we could laugh and cry with you. Mudbone, who broke the stereotypes that were so long held by white people about the black man, who was a character, not a caricature, who was a man, not a cartoon, who was not in blackface but a man with a black face. Mudbone was a genius and a player, a hustler and an honest man, a joker and a sentimental fool. You changed the way we viewed race. You changed the way we laughed. You changed the way America looked at Americans. You gave us new glasses. We could see ourselves as we actually were, just human and no different from each other, regardless of what color we were, who we loved, what we did, who we were, who we thought we were.

I owe a great debt to you, because I carry on what you did so beautifully, and I try to think, "What would Richard Pryor do?" Many comics follow in your footsteps, but you got the huge shoes to fill. I got some big feet, though, and I think I can do it. I am like a nasty Bigfoot Cinderella. Whenever I go on stage, I thank you, silently, in the dark velvet of the wings, because you gave me the blueprint of how to tell the truth and make it funny. You taught me to be a teacher, and I am there at school every day. Sometimes I get a shiny red apple on my desk. Humbly, my wish is to be the one who goes forth and continues your work. I want to carry your torch, and I will not set myself on fire. People who love you have said it. Seinfeld said to me once, "You are like Pryor at his best." It was a compliment I couldn't even get my head around. Who knew that this little, confused, sad, ugly, crazy, unwanted, unloved Korean American girl from the cloudy side of San Francisco could one day be compared to you? "I have a dream" are the only words that come to mind.

I am out of words. All that comes now is love and tears, and one last thank you.

Thank you.

the jeffersons

I had a fight with a man once when he said, "What everybody said about you is right. You are a selfish bitch, and you deserve to die alone." And what was strange about it was, I took it as a compliment. I was somewhat proud of the fact that I was selfish. Because to some men, the definition of selfish is that you don't think about them all the time. Well, then I am proud to be one selfish bitch. Why not hold your big, selfish hat with ostrich feathers and black net veil hanging over your face up high? And I don't care if I die alone. I'll probably be so out of my head that I won't even know who's around, so why would it matter if anybody's there or not. I'll just assume "anybody" is Sherman Helmsley.

I found *The Jeffersons* a particularly intense, subversively political sitcom that had quite an impact on me growing up, and still does to this day. I think my selfishness can be directly attributed to that show. The maid, Florence Johnston (played by Marla Gibbs), never did any work. Weezy Jefferson, the pampered wife (played by Isabel Sanford), with her comfy name, presumably a diminutive of "Louise," and her soft, generous body, led a life of leisure. Her silk jersey pantsuits and expensive furniture were a glowing advertisement for conspicuous consumption. For black America, *The Jeffersons* was a positive example of the new middle class, a first foray into formerly racially restricted territory. They were knocking down the walls of class and race, showing the possibility of the true definition of the American dream, "movin' on up." Of course there were conflicts, which were subtle yet loud bombs. There was an obvious yet unspoken competitive element between the Jeffersons and their neighbors, a racially mixed couple, the beautiful and elegant Helen Willis (played by Roxie Roker) and her white husband, ironically named "Tom" (Franklin Cover). Their style of living set the standard that the Jeffersons were constantly trying to meet, as even in friendship they were not immune to jealousy and envy. The Jeffersons, without examples of other people like them going before them, had to carve out an identity with the bits and pieces of what they knew of white culture and black upward mobility. George Jefferson, a self-made powder keg of inarticulate resentment, was constantly losing his temper and challenging the system, angry at the way upper-class African Americans were still not accorded upper-class privileges, even while paying upper-class rent. This raw angst was fueled by his own selfishness, which provided the axis of conflict within the story structure.

George rages at Florence, who no matter how much money he has made or what floor he has moved on up to, won't let him forget his race. His futile attempts to boss her around only serve as elaborate gags that always leave him with egg on his face, even if the egg happens to be the one Florence has dutifully prepared for his breakfast. Weezy was a comfort to George, and a barrier—sometimes even a physical one—between him and Florence. It was a war of what we were versus what we've become. Do we forget our roots when we move on up, or do we take them with us and continue to fight for racial equality? Do we have a responsibility to fight for those who still struggle for a piece of American pie, or can we merely savor what we have and let everyone else fend for themselves, and live in the penthouse of privilege without the guilt of obligation? Finally, has our own attainment of unprecedented affluence allowed us to ignore everyone we consider "less than" because it feels justified?

Then, of course, there is the beautiful and troubled Lionel (Mike Evans), adult son of the Jeffersons, romantically handicapped, culturally confused. Lionel represents the next step. Where are we going now? There's a nice view from up here, but you can look up or you can look down. What's your choice? Will you celebrate how far you have come, or will you look back, fatigued and bitter, at what a long journey it's been for you when others seemingly had such an easy time of it?

Selfishness is the right of all of us who struggle. That such introspection is depicted in a negative way is racism in action, as if self-realization—the dreaming of dreams, the achieving of goals, the living out the rewards—is bestowed upon the modest, the unambitious, the passive, the oblivious. Selfishness needs to be reclaimed as a tool for empowerment, so that we might all one day live in a world where class can transcend race, where the color of your skin does not affect the color of your money, or the color of the upholstery on your couch. That we are selfish gives us the opportunity to gain the power so that, in time, we might be selfless. To give back what we have learned. To teach what we know, and shorten the journey for those who will come after us. The one thing that really bothered me about *The Jeffersons,* though, was that British guy was always out in the hallway in his underwear. I still can't decipher the hidden meaning behind that.

how i loved you, michael

Michael Jackson has been the public freak for so long, it's not odd that he owns the Elephant Man's skeleton, unless he's sold it to defray court costs. Why does it still go on? Who are the people that want to cast him as the evil burgomaster who runs the village of terminally ill children who will either go into remission or get felt up while they lie asleep helpless in his bed? He said that stairs lead up to his bed, which makes me nervous because nobody should go up some stairs to get into a bed. You might go for a glass of water in the middle of the night and break your leg trying.

Is Michael Jackson worth this kind of media attention as phantom, bogeyman anymore—Jacko, the weirdo tabloid hero? What is the point of it now? I don't know what's going on. There are weird celebrities accused of murder (Phil Spector, Robert Blake) who don't undergo this type of public scrutiny. If they were to be as completely dissected by the media scalpel, I'm sure much more bizarre sound bites and makeup mania would surface. Why is it that Jackson's case is also very racially sensitive? No doubt, he is the undisputed King of Pop, and there's no one that can take away the glory of the past— who he was as a child star, and then his speed-of-light rise to fame and welcome journey to adulthood—the songs, the beats, the eloquence, *The Wiz*. I'm not being sarcastic. I love *The Wiz*. Nothing beats *The Wiz*. He took Brooke Shields to the Grammys, then Emmanuel Lewis, then Madonna. He was best friends with Elizabeth Taylor.

How does the public judge Jackson's racial identity? He seems to have tried to erase the race, so it would seem. Yet he really is still black, and there is tremendous emotional support from black artists who have come forward to speak of his influence on them. I always loved Michael Jackson. All the weirdness, too. But it's the music that made him unique and beautiful.

All in all, Michael Jackson may be the patron saint of celebrity insanity, but aren't we, the public, through constant finger pointing and accusing and indicting, for years and years, guilty too? Being the butt of jokes for so long can make anyone want to look like Enya.

See, I am doing it, too.

We are in the huge high school of life, and we bullied the odd kid because we became jealous of him, because we all knew that, inside, he had something so bright and beautiful we would never have, that we beat up on him instead. Is that the point of all this? It will be soon in the telling. The demise of Michael Jackson has been prophesized since the beginning of his career, and has reached a crescendo in the last decade.

How I loved Michael Jackson when I was young. When he was in the Jackson 5, I would watch them on our TV, which was made of wood and had the rabbit ears and we kept a baby pumpkin on the cabinet because the screen kept giving way to stripes and then we'd bang the pumpkin on the cabinet and usually that would fix it. What I saw, when it wasn't all striped, was this baby angel. This beautiful, dancing, singing little miracle. Like he was made by God, personally. You know them people that's so fine, you know that God personally took time out and made them Himself. Like they don't come out of the factory, you know, churned out, sometimes they look okay, but there always gonna be irregulars. Anyway, you looked at Michael Jackson and you saw that God did a good-ass job, probably even patted Himself on the back. Probably looked at Saint Peter and said, "Playa, playa, playa—check this out. This is the shit!"

I think God put Michael in a fucked-up family because sometimes that's what an artist needs—loneliness, struggle, abuse, pain—not all the time, but sometimes. When you grow up hard, there's gonna be some tears in your voice when you sing, you can reach out to all the other people who grew up hard who aren't artists and they can understand you. And they can feel like they aren't alone. Because thinking that you are the only one who feels bad is about the worst sadness there is. I heard all those tears in Michael's voice, but I also heard joy, and laughter. And hope. Which is what I needed then, because I, too, grew up hard. I wore out *Off the Wall* on my Mickey Mouse record player, listening to it over and over in my room, so I could drown out the sound of my parents fighting, so I could stop worrying about how I was going to get my ass kicked at school the next day, so I could stop thinking about my uncle's hands on me, touching where nobody needs to touch a little girl. I played it over and over and over and over. I stared at the cover. I kissed it. I put it next to my face. When I saw him, all grown up, with hands in his pockets, looking sly, having fun, with this smile so pretty nobody ever smiled as good before, he was the most beautiful thing in the whole world. I was just glad he was real. He was out there in the world somewhere. He may be drinking a Pepsi, or out on a date, or watching TV, or eating a corn on the cob— but he existed. This knowledge kept me going through the bad shit of being a kid. Not that I thought I'd ever meet him or anything. It just gave me so much love to know that someone could be that beautiful and perfect, and it seemed like he had good manners. It gave me this fever dream that maybe one day I would grow up and be like that. Be so beautiful and talented that I made kids who grew up hard want to keep going, because maybe one day they could grow up and be like me. I did. Michael helped me do it.

I got older, and so did he. He changed. The hyperbolic chamber, the Elephant Man skeleton, the plastic surgery, the nose that was not there anymore, the race erased by the vitiligo, the disease that made him whiter and whiter and made him look more like Lesley-Anne Down every day. Michael—what happened? You were there for me. I don't know if I can repay my debt to you, for what your music gave me. I hope Liz Taylor is there for you. I hope that monkey is still around, or is he dead? I can't remember. I don't know what you did to those children. I ask nothing, I accuse nothing. I only say that you helped this child to grow up into a woman, to be fully alive, to not only survive but thrive. Thank you for that. I dare anyone now to go listen to "She's Out of My Life" and not cry like a bitch.

i love hip-hop

I love hip-hop. It's a language that speaks to me, with the complexity of the beats, the dexterity of the rhymes, the posture and pride of rappers who make me swoon. It's like opera to me, with all the Wagnerian Sturm und Drang, but with modern values and transformative knowledge. My newest obsession is the Neptunes' song "Pop Shit." I've never heard anything so beautiful in my life. The layering of the samples, the vocal harmony perfectly dovetailing with the MC's swagger, there's small heaven in that song. I believe that we get complimentary snack-size portions of the afterlife, and we all receive them in a different way. For me, it's the arrogant smirk in Pharrell Williams's voice, the skittish percussion and the dizzying freak I get on whenever I hear that song.

The overture that captured me for life was Public Enemy's "Don't Believe the Hype." In the late '80s, I worked at Stormy Leather, a leather dyke emporium on Howard Street in San Francisco. Sundays, it was quiet, and we'd listen to a radio station that ran Malcolm X and Martin Luther King Jr. speeches over phat beats, which felt like the birth of something great. Word was born, and the DJ would spin you right into Chuck D.'s booming voice. There was such truth to rap right then, and there were no apologies made to anyone about anything. It was the first time it struck me that music could be political, even though I had grown up in San Francisco at the tail end of the Summer of Love; musicians then were rebelling against their own establishment, and even though there were also amazing poets, their rhymes didn't affect me like the epics of Afrika Bambattaa or Grandmaster Flash. Who gives a fuck about *Howl*? What was it supposed to mean, anyway? Wasn't that dude in NAMBLA?

Chuck D. I took to as my new leader. His righteous anger and eloquence was infectious, the beats hypnotic, the passionate struggle of not only people of color but really of all minorities was expressed in his lyrics. I got it. We all got it at Stormy Leather, toiling over the sheets of black leather, the scent getting into our skin, as we bobbed our heads. We understood oppression—as below-the-poverty-line women, as queer, as Asian, Latino and Black. Not only that, as sex workers we were vilified by feminists as traitors to our own movement, since sadomasochism was viewed as accommodation and supplication to the patriarchy. We were also blasted by the queer establishment for wearing chaps, and making the entire GLBT constituency look like perverts. Like *we* were the ones in NAMBLA.

For the first time, we got to make our shame into rage, and rap gave us the formula, the *pi,* for our feelings of misery and displacement, which before went unanswered, an equation burning in our just-born political brains. Yes, Public Enemy was talking about the ghetto, but we all lived in the ghetto no matter what our address. In the projects of the mind, 911 is, and always will be, a joke. It would take a nation of millions to hold us back. The revolution will not be televised. I am a black man, and I will never be a veteran.

Things turned around when Ice Cube released "Black Korea," a wrathful, venomous anthem against the Korean merchants of the inner city. I felt like I was cast out of a tribe that I so desperately needed to belong to. Gangsta rap, still powerful, had sexist themes that I blocked out because I still wanted to have that hardness, something that would exist as a melodic talisman inside me when the "rainbow was enuf." I was partly in agreement, because the song was about people I knew, relatives who had banished me years ago, so there was an odd satisfaction to it, but, then again, my face I could not camouflage, even though my mind belonged behind enemy lines. I also felt that kind of weirdness you feel when someone makes fun of your mom—a sense of propriety, like, "I can say that but you can't." Also, the undeniable violence and racism of the song made an indelible mark on my precious amulet, and it just felt like bad luck. Ice Cube eventually apologized for the song, and made the genius film *Friday,* yet that same antagonism between Koreans and blacks exists, in a mythological realm, in that neighborhood between *Do the Right Thing* and South Central during the riots.

I don't care.

I still love hip-hop.

There isn't the kind of unifying political message there once was, but there's unending beauty, which grows despite all the maleness, materialism, misogyny, malevolence toward homosexuals, mayhem, murder and yachts. The rhymes are still rebellious, and the styles have become sophisticated beyond what anyone could have ever imagined. Nothing is perfect, but the first heady years, when Sundays were all about Chuck D. and the world that we, the freaks of all freaks, were bound to inherit and hopefully come to rule, but, unlike our predecessors, would do with truth, compassion, justice and generosity, gave us an enduring hope that keeps Public Enemy on my iPod to this day. Fight the power.

FEMINISM IS A FEMINIST ISSUE

"so if you are not a feminist,

kill yourself."

Feminism is nonnegotiable.

If you are not a feminist, you do not deserve to live.

Do you think you grew out of the ground? That the stork dropped you off? You fell from a tree? NO. You came out of a woman. And even if your mother was awful, abandoned you, abused you, ignored you, made you hate yourself, put you on a diet at age six so that, to this day, you still have a complex about your weight, molested you, competed with you, made you join a cult, was jealous of you, was nicer to your brother than you, sewed you matching outfits, made you eat liver or any other kind of organ meat (or, like my mom, dried fish!), gave you a Toni home perm, made you as crazy as she, did not love you—you still owe her your life. You would not be here if it were not for her. I'm not telling you that you have to do anything for your mom. I'm just saying we need to respect women for the fact that they are where the world begins. They are the reason we are still here, and will continue to be here. Forever.

So if you are not a feminist, kill yourself.

Normally, I do not advocate suicide, but this time you do not have a choice. You do not have the right to live on this planet, and you need to kill yourself and go to your misogynist heaven, which is much like the Playboy Mansion, where you can read all sorts of men's magazines like *Maxim, FHM, Stuff, Hustler, Gear* and, of course, *Playboy,* except . . . there will be no women there. No real T & A, just paper cuts and those annoying subscription cards that fall out all over the place, because since you did not appreciate the wonder of what T & A really is, and because you did not understand the importance of us being here, your exploitation of them makes you eligible for a hell where we are not there at all. Kind of like jail, but you do not get to make other inmates your bitch.

And then you have to read the articles. That is what I call Hades. Pussy, pussy, everywhere, but not a drop to . . .

What people need to understand is that the pussy is the Front Door of Life. Do you get that? Nobody really thinks about it like that up in the dusty ancient cabinet of old white men that think they know everything. Woman has the right to let someone in, or to tell them to come back another time, or even to have a sign that says NO SOLICITORS.

Woman has the right to be exalted, cherished and respected.

Woman has the right to choose, to choose for herself, for her own body, for her own life.

Feminism is nonnegotiable. Word to your mother.

crazy eyes

Body dysmorphia has got to go. This is this ignant disease where you don't know what you look like. It's similar to another condition that I believe is called "crazy eyes"—not the way that other people see you ("Look at that fool Marty Feldman—he's got some crazy eyes!"), but the way you see yourself. The insanity, which we use as our vision, surfaces when we get dressed to go somewhere where we think people will be looking at us with the same crazy eyes that we have. There is a cure for this disease, but, sadly, people don't really think that it works. The cure is, nobody cares what you look like except you and your crazy eyes. It's a tough pill to swallow, like a horse pill you have to take with a gallon of Sparklett's to get the whole thing down, and even then it just sticks in your throat, creating a pharmaceutical Adam's apple. That's nasty, thinking that nobody cares what you look like except you, but that's because they're too busy looking at themselves, thinking about what's wrong with them and dealing with their own crazy eyes. And even if they do care about what you look like, it's only a momentary, fleeting thought, a brief overview and comparison between what you look like against what they think they look like, so the thought isn't really about you, it's about them and their crazy eyes, not you and your crazy eyes. So fuck it. You're both crazy, and that's final.

Crazy eyes is not fatal, but it can lead to other diseases that are. It is a gateway to other diseases, just like marijuana is a gateway to other drugs, and the "munchies," which is a gateway to crazy eyes. If left untreated, crazy eyes will get worse, and could develop into disordered eating, which leads to the wonderful world of Bulimarama (Try 'em all! Bulimarexia, Good Ol' Binge'n'Purge, Exercise Bulimia, Laxative Bulimia, "I'm starting my diet tomorrow so I have to get it all in before midnight" Bulimia, Honey Mustard Bulimia) and the Grim Reaper, Anorexia, coming to claim the lives of young women, much like consumption did in the Victorian era. She's a tall, gaunt figure, chic and wiry, draped in black muslin, but instead of a scythe this skeleton has a fork and spoon, because even death thinks you need a good hearty meal of macaroni and cheese to fortify you for your long journey into the afterlife.

And then, what if you die before you reach your goal weight of forty-five pounds? Perhaps your narrow-ass ghost will be condemned to roam the metropolitan shopping malls of your past, like the poor old prisoners who, even in death, refuse to leave their cells on Alcatraz. Will the dressing-room doors in Urban Outfitters creak open, then slam shut, for no reason? Supernatural shrieks coming from inside the slatted stalls, "I NEED A LARGER SIZE!!!!!!!!!! AHHH-HHHHHHHH!!!!!!!!!! HELPPPPPP MEEEEEEEEEE!!!!!!!!!!" as clerks rush in and find nobody there, nothing but the lingering scent of almond vomit, a chill in the air and a size 0 pair of Frankie B. jeans turned inside out on the floor.

Or maybe you will find your way to heaven. God knows, you

deserve it, having put yourself through a correspondence course in hell, getting your GED in suffering in the precious few days of your tragic life, all the while maintaining a rigorous workout schedule and an insufficient caloric intake. Will the first thing you ask when you reach the Pearly Gates, which, thankfully for you, is atop an impossibly long flight of cement steps, be, "Where's the gym?"

Crazy eyes is wildly contagious. Everybody has some form of it. The people who pick and choose the images that we see daily on TV, in movies, in magazines and advertising—everywhere—have the craziest eyes of all, which is why this malady is worse than most other forms of biological warfare. Smallpox's got nothing on CE. Crazy eyes is the ultimate weapon of mass destruction because it works slowly, eroding the mind and the spirit and eventually the body, pound by pound, inch by inch, and it sets its crazy sights upon young women, who provide the gateway to future generations. If crazy eyes escalated to pandemic proportions, which is the next level up from the epidemic we have now, there would be a massive shortage of females capable of reproduction. Even if all of us didn't die right away from CE, and the diseases caused by CE infection, low body weight would make menstruation impossible, and procreation rare and difficult. This, along with the few remaining fertile women unwilling to become pregnant because they don't want to look "fat," would eventually kill off the human race altogether.

And today, with the advent of the Internet, and the crazy eyes of the media enforcing their crazy vision on the global optic nerve, as the world gets smaller through technology, becomes more and more uniform in its tastes, customs, practices, beliefs, ideals, collective dreams and nightmares—as cultures homogenize and pasteurize and become one solid block of cheese nobody is going to eat—crazy eyes will spread faster than a wildfire in Granada Hills. Don't act like I'm some crackpot who is about to put this manifesto on a sandwich board and walk up and down the Third Street Promenade with a megaphone and those joke glasses with the eyeballs on springs popping out. You know crazy eyes is real. You have probably suffered from it at some time in your life. I'm a CE survivor, and I live in fear for others who may not have the strength or even the reason to save themselves.

There is hope. Crazy eyes is even easier to fix than astigmatism or glaucoma. You don't even need to get laser surgery on your retinas. Prevention is the best line of defense. When you look at yourself in the mirror, you can say only one thing: "I look fine." Do not think about what you ate today or yesterday—or ever. Do not change your outfit. Do not say anything about yourself to yourself. Do not think about the way you look again. Think instead about how nice it is that somebody loves you, or that your dog is so sweet when she follows the sunlight as it moves across the sky, napping at every window with such regularity that you could set your watch by her gentle snores and dog dreams, or that you miss someone and maybe you should call them, or if you can't call them because they are not around anymore think about how much you loved them and why, or how much you hated them and why, or about how the thoughts of love or hate can be equally provocative and tantalizing, or that sometimes there really is an easy way to do things, or that popcorn is always a good thing to get at the movies, or that you can stay home and watch TV if you want to, not even committing to a specific show—just flipping for no reason except that you want to, or that it's weird that certain colors are called that, like why is blue called blue?—or whatever ignant or smart or sad or stupid or funny or brilliant or ridiculous thought to fill your mind with instead of "Do I look okay?"

Stop crazy eyes before it starts. You look fine.

why must i bleed alone?

I take this new birth control pill where one of the side effects is having four menstrual periods a year. It's menopause in a pinch! I feel like an Olympic gymnast or some other kind of professional athlete, too muscular and stressed out for feminine luxuries such as menses and the prom. When it comes time for one of my quarterly sheds, it takes me by surprise, and I welcome it like a long lost friend. We have lots of euphemisms for menstruation, and we don't refer to it unless in the company of women—and rarely even then.

I had a friend who was absolutely intolerant of anyone complaining about her period. She'd never had cramps or heavy bleeding or stopping then mysteriously restarting or accidents or a missed period in her life, and she staunchly believed that no one else should either. If it were mentioned in her presence, through clenched teeth she reminded one and all of her manageable monthly flow and freedom from pain, and change the subject.

Then there are the judgmental ones. I have been around the alternative-healing community for decades, and when confiding in friends/amateur healers/shamans about my woman's issues, they would almost always launch into a tirade against wheat or dairy or white sugar or caffeine. When doubled over and obsessing about banana chocolate chip muffins, the last thing on my mind is yoga. Lectures about my bad health and spiteful shaming usually greet any attempt on my part to have learned discourse about menstruation, and so the best way to get a grip on it was to get rid of it the best that I could.

It is strange how little talk there is about our periods, as if the subject, if not in a health and wellness context, were morally reprehensible. It is a dirty business that we women keep to ourselves. But why are we so secretive? Over half the world menstruates at one time or another, but you'd never know it. Isn't that strange?

I was thirteen when I first got my period. My mother was not overjoyed. She gave me big, foamy white Kotex pads that she had still left over from before her hysterectomy. They were old, so they had long tabs on either end for the sanitary belt that was supposed to keep it on. When I put the whole contraption on, I looked like a sumo wrestler. Usually, I couldn't be bothered putting the weird belt together, so the pad, without its newfangled modern adhesive that was meant to secure the wad inside your pants, would slip and slide all around my area, creating something akin to a potato-print card. My mother showed me how to dispose of the pads. She folded them up, wrapped them in toilet paper, shoved them inside a paper bag, crumpled up the bag into a ball, then buried it deep inside the bathroom trash. She repeated the process twice for me, miming the steps the second time so as not to waste any of those gigantic pads. There was incredible shame in the whole business of bleeding, and she wanted me to be painfully aware of it. The shame could work to my benefit, because if ever I wanted to get out of doing something I could just cry "Period!" and it was an instant no-contest. It was like the magic word. Everybody left me alone.

Of course, I was incredibly lax about throwing those huge pads away, and my negligence was punished with more lessons on how to properly dispose of them, as if they were radioactive nuclear waste. My father even started to shout about my lackadaisical, unsanitary sanitary pad refuse, but he never really completed the thought because I think he realized, midscream, that he was out of his jurisdiction. My father didn't talk much, anyway. If anything, he hollered. But, even then, he was brief. Korean parents are like that. It is appropriate and traditional for parents to show no discernible affection or emotion toward their children. My father was positively textbook when it came to this. My mother was too watery, too in love with the French, too mommy, to comply. My father said maybe five things during my entire childhood and adolescence that I remember, one being unprompted and very odd. I had just come home from school one day and was walking up to my room when he shouted, "You will never use tampons." That was it. Wow. Thanks, Dad. Words to live by. This was during the big Rely toxic shock syndrome scare, which vied with the Hillside Strangler as women's number one fear. Toxic shock was ominous because they never really said how you got it, or why, or what happened when you did get it. It just struck you dead in the cunt. It had the combined qualities of a nuclear fallout warning and a stalker-rapist on the loose. What an awful joke that name Rely was! As if women who dared rely on anything would be duly punished.

My monthly flow staged its own rebellion. I constantly bloodied my sheets with robust flamboyance. My bed often took the appearance of the scene of a crime. My mother would wash the sheets without a word, and the secrecy around the curse kept me from having to do laundry ever. When I became a comic, it was drilled into me by several other women comics that we should never talk about our periods. Male comics often stereotyped female comics and dismissed them because "all they do is talk about their periods." Talking about menstruation became tantamount to a black person eating watermelon. We just couldn't do it. Even now, I'm a bit ashamed when I must disclose that I menstruate at all. It's probably because since I don't truly menstruate anymore, it gives me enough distance from it to voice my once hidden thoughts about it. What's the deal? Why must I feel like I bleed alone? Or that I once bled alone?

my mother

I really, really, really, really love my mother. It's not the best between my family and me. There are so many crimes left unpunished, debts unpaid, white elephants in the middle of the room that no one will even offer a peanut to. We are in the red, emotionally speaking. But with my mother, things are easy, flexible. She bends and moves with grace, and even though she is barely five feet tall she looms over me still.

There are lots of things you don't know about her. She speaks French like a Parisian, because she was one for many years. In the early '60s, she kept a tiny bedsit in the City of Lights and taught classes to foreign students. She had her hair flipped and wore heavy black eyeliner above her upper lashes, just like Brigitte Bardot's. After I was born, she spent many hours designing clothes for me. The best I remember was a red wool coat and dress set, trimmed with black mink, with a matching pillbox hat. She liked the way that Jackie Kennedy had such understated elegance, and so she felt that it was only right that I should have the same.

Even though she made all my clothes, she never fell into the awful trap young mothers do at times of making matching mother-daughter outfits. My mother thought that to be gauche and beneath our stature, for we were going to be future fashion icons. We didn't really get to do that because she had to work so hard at the little snack bar my parents ran then, and the dresses were fewer and farther between. She kept drawings of amazing gowns, gowns that would exist in theory only, and bolts of cloth unused in cabinets. After I got married, the sewing machine was sent to me, but it was too complex for me to use. I still sew everything laboriously by hand, but I make my own things, which are unique and lovely, just like she taught me.

My mother loves gigantic jewelry, and keeps the most valued pieces wrapped in toilet paper in a Folger's coffee can. She is most fond of amber, especially the variety that is opaque and honey yellow, and she wraps her neck with long strings of beads of different sizes and hues.

When my mother dreams, she flies, and she loves it. She says she visits me often in these dreams, flying over my house, over her sisters' houses all the way on the other side of the world, seeing all of us from above, sending us love and whatever good things she remembers to bring along before she goes to bed. She worries because she's not sure that I'm happy, and she's right about that sometimes, but that can't always be helped, which maybe is just the way things are in life. She accepts this, but flies over the cities she loves most nonetheless: Frankfurt, Hong Kong, Seoul, Paris, New York.

My mother is an accomplished flamenco guitarist, completely self-taught. I don't know who dances for her. I can't picture my father in tight black pants, red rose clenched between his teeth, but you can never really know your parents. They're your parents, and they're not meant to be much more than that, unless you're very special and get to have your parents also as your friends, but even then there is a limit to this intimacy, borders not to be crossed. Flamenco dancing, or even the tango, are not the type of secrets that get disclosed between mother and child.

My mother had surgery on her heart. She's fine, and was discharged from the hospital in a day or so. Yet there were many hours when we didn't know if she would be fine. Many slow, terrible minutes were spent waiting by the phone. I could do little but sit down, stand up, then sit down again. Well-meaning friends, insistent on helping me, wore me down even further. The Rescuers, like the little mice with berets on their heads, were infuriated at their own inability to do anything to ease my worry. There were lots of bad thoughts, scary visions, sweet memories and crying—oh, lots of crying.

I don't think I have ever heard my father so scared in my life. He downplayed his alarm with false laughter, and by turning off his cell phone "by accident." He makes me angry because the bridge I burned so long ago between us will have to be rebuilt, hurriedly, and that's hard to do. He has been in love with my mother for over forty years, and even though he has not been particularly good at anything having to do with love at least he was still there, sleeping in the waiting room, all through that long night. Even though I disowned him and was adopted by a lovely, lively, brilliant painter-poet-writer-historian, tattoo aficionado gay father, I have to take him back, because he's trying, and that's going to have to be good enough for now.

If you have parents that you like, or one parent that you like, enjoy it. Remember that whatever happens, it's okay, that they're okay, that everything that's part of life is okay, because life is life and life is okay. Always.

my mother's heart

My mother's heart is small. Its borders reach out much farther than the tiny nation of her body. If you picture Monaco, then try to fit all of North America including Canada, even Quebec, into that miniscule, opulent kingdom, then you have it about right.

My husband drove my brother and me to see her. She was up, on her feet, quickly, albeit slightly less quickly than before, padding around her huge, slightly spare home, filled with photographs and massage machines of every caliber—kind of like an elderly version of *Toys in Babeland,* with odd lumbar pillows everywhere, the physically fortifying detritus of the aged.

My parents adore my husband, for it gives them a deep feeling of relief, an interior solidity and gratitude, that they have not completely failed me in my upbringing. Since they can't attribute any of my artistic and financial achievements to themselves—wrongfully so, for I would not be this insane had it not been for the chaotic universe that once was my childhood—they look to my husband as a gentle savior, which he is, but not in the ways they think he is. I don't care; they love him and that's what matters. When my father tells a man who is not Korean, who is white, who is not a lawyer or a doctor and doesn't play golf, that he loves him, that he has been blessed with another son, that he must be addressed as "Daddy" or temper tantrums may erupt un-expectedly, it's worth it—at least to me. It's my parents' failure that brought me the artistic humility and grace that would make my own failure impossible, so I guess I have to thank them.

I found a scribbled note stuffed in my mother's purse, no doubt when she dashed, by herself, to the hospital. In a frightened and almost unintelligible script, she made a treasure map to all the jewelry hidden in the house, to give to me and only me. She doesn't keep it in some pretty box, hiding it instead as if there's a war still on, which, ironically, there is.

The jewelry is hidden in the oddest places, which I won't disclose here, only to say that I also have picked up this odd habit, except I used to hide drugs the same way. My hiding places now will be filled with her precious jewels. They are the most important things in the world to her, and to me, and not because they are valuable; the money spent on them is not why they are so protected. My aunt's ring and necklace are fashioned of emeralds and diamonds, broken off the crown of some deposed princess, and made just for my mommy, the true Queen, a gift of thanks—unbelievable gratitude to my mother, when she was the only one in the family who could take care of my aunt's father as he lay dying. The rest of the family was consumed with grief, too paralyzed to carry their paralyzed father to his bed, too teary-eyed to drive to the hospital day after day, too shattered to secure a burial plot and comfort him through the terribly painful eclipse of life, as the soul slowly leaves the body, and even though my mother was not his biological daughter she was his son's wife, the only one to step up to be the midwife in his death.

The jewelry is mine now. I'm fucking wearing it, and don't think for a second that I'm not gonna wear it all at the same time—that's right, biaaatch!!! I'm wearing my aunt's pearl necklace—my Kun Immo—who died far above the world, halfway between the hospital and her home, aboard a plane over Seattle. Before she died, she promised my mother this pearl, and during the divvying up of all her beautiful things—my aunt was not only a beauty herself but sur-rounded herself with beauty, big-ass beauty—it somehow got lost. But the pearl, my mother knew, was the most important of the jewelry, and it was hers. She would not leave without it. She looked under every couch pillow, picked through every pocket, emptied every purse, turned that motherfucker of a house inside out—everything— until she found it hidden in a tiny zippered pouch in an old handbag.

The pearl necklace is mine now, too. It hangs directly over my heart, and this heart is now a fortress of jewels, over a century's worth of the history of the women of my family, their love expressed through their rings and necklaces, pendants and earrings. Things they were not able to buy themselves but were given by their husbands, and, therefore, were all they had to give, but it means everything. Because of this history, this jewelry is powerful; yes, a bracelet can move a mountain. I'll show you sometime.

My mother gave me all of it, bags and bags of it, because she doesn't want to keep it anymore hidden away, like our history, our stories left untold, for these jewels and their stories are my inheritance. They can't be appraised. If I brought them to the *Antiques Roadshow,* they would throw them back in my face. Some of it is plastic, some of it is fake, some shit came from QVC, and then there are souvenirs from seaside honeymoons at the turn of the century, happy times, terrible times, then, now. But its value surpasses all the money in the world. It isn't bling. It's love, this long, long love that these sisters had for each other, with hands reaching across the sea, even though separated by continents and hardship—war, immigration and isolation, war, racism and hatred in the new land, war, loneliness and death, war, madness and suicide, war, cancer and AIDS and Alzheimer's, war, a little peace, and then the bad marriages of the '70s. And now another war.

I am now the keeper of the ring. And the brooch, and the bangles. Don't fuck with me.

dinkies

The last fingers on each of my hands are so small that they can't even rightfully be called "pinkies" because they are even smaller than that. They are more like "dinkies," and usually they are not noticed for a long time, because, normally, unless you are shopping for an engagement ring or getting a manicure your hands don't get eyeballed in a way that makes it clear that you're a finger freak. I have dinkies so small it is as if one joint were missing, as if it is just two parts instead of all three, but the parts are intact, and supposedly it's a family trait and not a deformity, although when trying to call attention to myself I would claim that it was the result of a rare disease or bone disorder in an attempt to appear more glamorous.

The last person in my family to have "the finger" was my great-great-grandmother, who was a notorious and riotous great wildebeest of a woman. She had the blackest hair, which she never cut and wore in a tight bun at the base of her neck. Her hair remained midnight black until her death, at the age of 122! Her laugh was loud, and could be heard from miles away, even in other villages. Although Koreans are a staunch, deliberately arrogant patriarchy, and unwavering in their commitment to it, everybody—even the biggest men—were scared of this giantess with black hair and tiny dinky pinkies. She wore pants, and nobody even commented on it, which is an incredible thing, considering the customs of the village she lived in.

The legend of her ugliness spread far and wide, and people traveled many miles in pilgrimage, if only to catch a glimpse of her and stand in awe of what they considered to be some kind of holy error, yet she wore her massive features and bull-in-a-china-shop personality like a badge of honor. Smoking her corncob pipe, she held her family together during terrible times. She had an unfailingly good nature, but was rumored to have killed people with her bare hands, using just four fingers on each, in order to protect her precious children, her sisters, her brothers, her husband, whom she loved with voluptuous passion, ravenously and overwhelmingly, since he treated her exactly as she was, a warrior and a goddess, a love that defied the conventions of the time, and lasted for more than a century. Even random people in her village were privy to her protection. Her power was legendary, and she was generous with it, because she saw her village as an extension of herself; like her hair, it grew and grew, and it was all hers, held tightly at the back of her head, a symbol of unity in a world filled with strife. The town's inability to judge her for her eccentricity, her famous "ugliness," her trousers and her ever-smoking pipe, her unabashed defiance of convention, tradition and sexual persona, was an astonishing feat of heroic confidence in her true identity.

Through war and famine, daughters kidnapped by soldiers and put into service as "comfort women" (sexual slaves who would be kept in tents to satisfy the troops, which doesn't sound all that comfortable) through the years in refugee camps, lost pages of history, stories so painful they have been deleted from the family archives, tales that I can't seem to extract from anyone in my family, secrets kept so long, padlocks of shame rusted and useless, the keys no longer able to pry them open: All they remember is her, and they grasp my fingers, my oddly tiny dinky pinkies, and see that she has returned. She is still here. To protect them. Hold them. Love them. Her raucous laughter fills their ears, and they hold my hands long and hard, and sometimes tears come, which I do not or cannot ever understand.

I wasn't there, but I have this biological legacy to live up to her legend, to carry on her work, of compassion, protection, defiance and laughter, since she isn't here to do it herself. To grow my hair and not be afraid of my village's judgment and ridicule, of my "ugliness," hugeness, my inability to conform, my indelicate manner, my loud and resounding laugh, my passion and unfailing and infallible strength, my need to wear pants, figuratively as well as literally. That my hands are small makes no difference. I have the power of the whole world in them.

courtney love

I do want to be a good feminist. I really do. But I worry about the state of the female nation. For instance: Courtney Love. Everything she does raises the stakes on the celebrity-death pools, and brings out all the people who "love to hate" her.

This is unfair. I was speaking to another feminist, whose opinion I hold in high regard, and she admitted, quite casually, that she hated Courtney Love. When pressed for a reason why, she stammered, not realizing that she might be taken to task for her own misogyny. She couldn't come up with anything acceptable, only "I just love to hate her." But why? Courtney Love is an incredible artist who has endured public derision and scorn for well over a decade. What man could survive that? Yet in any real way, the feminist majority has yet to come to her defense. No one has come forward with the simple question "Why is it that I am hating another woman with such ease?"

I admit, I have always had a real soft spot for Courtney Love. Perhaps it is my own wonder at the nature of rock, how it attracts shape-
shifters and gift-grifters, how it manages to eat its young, generation
after generation. Maybe it is an appetite for destruction, my Guns N'
Roses nature, how I will always have a side to me that is a rough
downhill run, the kind where you start and can't stop and pretty soon
you're exceeding your own speed limit, and there is no end to it but
an utterly bitter scalding by concrete. Courtney Love has been running downhill for over a decade, and there are many hurdles in her
path. I suspect she is the Keith Richards of my generation, the one
who will beat the odds and win every watercooler wager as the bottle-
blonde-with-dark-roots dark horse simply by staying alive. But the
Rolling Stone spokes-addict for kidney dialysis never had to contend
with misogyny, which Love has had to bear unrelentingly, without the
support of the feminist community at all.

I want to know why this hatred is casual and unquestioned. Her
behavior is too embarrassing and unpredictable for any dot-org to
get behind—I understand that. She is the eternal Underdog that
never trumps Overcat. But Courtney Love has made significant
contributions to the mythology of the rock star, and changed the
standards for women in rock. However, her work as a musician is
rarely, if ever, brought up when speaking about her. It is always about
the drug arrests, the lack of grace in her social interactions, the possibility that she might have killed her husband—a theory supported
by many, including her own father, the author of two books on the
subject.

In fact, there was a whole movie made—Nick Broomfield's astonishingly inventive *Kurt and Courtney*—attempting to prove/disprove her guilt and/or complicity in her husband's suicide and/or murder. It's an illuminating work because it reveals the extent of the intense distrust for women that exists in society. What Broomfield's documentary shows is the doom left in the wake of a woman who defies all definition of a widow: a rocker, a starlet, an icon and a mother. She manages to be all these things anyway and then some. Underneath all the circumstantial evidence and theory presented by Broomfield, what is undeniable is that the documentary is proof that the world abhors women, and this hatred is as natural as Mother Nature herself. When given a choice, we are going to assume guilt over innocence, evil over good, when it comes to the ladies. Always. Without exception. Every time. The thesis statement, broken down to the barest essentials, is that chicks suck, and everyone says, "Ho!!!!!"

No one ever talks about the cool brilliance of Courtney Love's latest record. They speak about her with the distance and superiority of the eternal judge, the tsk-tsk of the outside observer, who coolly and impassively watches the events of everything unfold from afar, always detached, always removed.

Why is this okay? If you are a feminist or not, I don't think it is acceptable to hate a woman in the media unless you have a well-worked-out explanation as to why, have examined all your own prejudices and can convince me that you are not just another fascist follower of fashion. I don't care if that is a sexist notion; it forces the burden of guilt on the jury's shoulders. Individually, we must be called upon to prove our suspicion, to put our feelings into words. If you are going to triple her bail, that is the least we can do for her.

martha stewart

I'm not a homemaker by any stretch of the imagination. If there are panty hose on the floor in the living room, that is where they are supposed to be. If the DVD library has the wrong disc in each case, it's like that for a reason. It's my own personal Dewey decimal system. I like having food plates out for several days in a row, and they *do* belong on the nightstand. They help me to go to sleep. And vermin are adorable!

I'm not a Martha fan. I know that I am weird and possess the most bizarre taste in décor; my interiors should reflect my interior, and mine do. The very thought of a rolling pin makes my carpal tunnel ache and pop. I do have a craft-oriented side, but it is driven by iron-on-patch pajamas and customized stripper thongs, nothing too challenging.

Yet, I cannot believe the injustice that Martha Stewart has faced. Just because I don't embrace pastels, especially that light mint/sage that she loves so much, it doesn't mean that I would turn my back on her. I don't understand anything about the world of big business—strategic planning, mission statements, financing: this is for people who wear suits or suntan panty hose, who sit in fluorescent light all day, who have in-boxes and office affairs. I have never worked in an office, so I don't know anything about it. But I do know that Martha Stewart never did anything worse than what her male counterparts do on a daily basis.

It seems to me that America inherently hates it when women are wildly successful, and there is a built-in punishment that comes along with that kind of wealth. I can't follow a recipe for shit, but I can spot misogyny from miles away. Why do we hate women who beat all the odds and come out on top? Why are books written to "expose" their financial "deviance," as well as their "ambitchiness"?

Martha Stewart was promoting the idea of perfection, wherever you could have it. It was about that notion of perfecting something, and then it becoming yours. This was the American Dream as it could be made accessible to American women. You could empower yourself through action, and that is probably the danger that Martha Stewart represents. She is the authority on independence, and that is what we don't want from our mothers or for our daughters.

You can't wear a burqa or tie raffia properly. You need freedom and a wide table if you want to make your own marshmallows or liquid soap from scratch (I have no idea why anyone would want to make anything from scratch, but that's beside the point). The thought that putting Martha away for a time was some kind of blow to the misogynist family structure is dangerous.

The real point is that America doesn't like women who are powerful and successful and not nice about it. She went to jail for being a bitch. I'm glad I wasn't on trial, because I would be serving consecutive life sentences. I would be throwing my last meal of fried chicken and Pepsi at the guards before being escorted by the chaplain to my lethal injection. I would refuse to take the governor's call.

Big deal. She wasn't a nice lady. Personality faults should not be worth a jail sentence. Even after she got out of jail, they made her wear one of those cuffs around her leg, like she was Suge Knight. Her magazine *Living* might be so boring that it would make you *not* want to go on living, but I don't think Martha is capable of popping a cap in anyone's ass.

I never want to have ecru chenille slipcovers or homemade beeswax candles scented with lavender from my own garden, but I do believe the unceremonious denial of Martha Stewart's freedom should make us seriously question our own.

all hail tha queen

I remember when I first met Queen Latifah. It was in San Francisco at a huge benefit for AIDS awareness in the early '90s. She was walking out of the green room, and her bodyguard, a large, imposing man, straight-armed me to get out of the Queen's way, and then she saw me, recognized me immediately and embraced me warmly. "Oh, I have been wanting to meet you, gurrrl—you are funny! How you doin'? My name is Dana." I was shaking, and couldn't even muster up the courage to say anything. I just stood there and gaped. She smiled at me warmly, and went on stage. She was there with the cast of *Living Single,* and showing much love to a worshipful crowd.

My ex-girlfriend, who I still believe is mad at me for breaking up with her, after fifteen or so years, my shit is that tight—for real, tho'— was obsessed with the Queen, and made me a mixed tape with the single "U.N.I.T.Y," and to this day when I hear that song's bittersweet hook, a war cry for all girls who want the respect that is due to them, that they have had enough of the gender war, the male bonding that left them cold and alone in an already hostile world, I am brought to my knees in reverie. She truly is the Queen, but not just in name; her undeniable power and grace can come only from a true royalty that only God can bestow, a Queen from the true kingdom. There is no one that even comes close to her in terms of talent, charisma, beauty—who cares about the breast reduction and the weight loss, which could be construed by some as a self-betrayal of her original spirit, the natural largesse of her being? She had some back problems, so get over it. I don't have to assume a feminist stance in judging what one might do with one's own body, and when it comes to the Queen nobody and nothing can knock her off her throne.

I got a big chest of drawers myself, and am not really a bra wearer because I am a member of SAG and AFTRA, if you know what I'm sayin', and one day in Victoria's Secret—where I will never go again, by the way, and was only there because I was bored at the airport with a long-ass layover—I was talking to my man on my cell, having a half fight because of missing each other and neither wanting to admit it, and the saleswoman was holding up a support bra and pointing at it wildly, desperately trying to do something about the fact that my breasts were not as jacked up as she thought they should be, so she needed to give me some of that titty sign language, like "The only way you gonna keep that man of yours is if you shove that shit up to your chin!!!"—all frantic and crazed like she was about to shout "UNDERWIRE!!!!!" in a crowded movie theater. I didn't need that from her and promptly left the store while still on the phone. Bras don't make me feel good. They hurt my back, and I could care less about where my breasts are as long they are still on my body. I'm not going jogging anywhere, nor do I have a set of lingerie that matches because who has the time to wash that shit separately or put anything in a fishnet bag before you do—and, I'm sorry, I just don't care that much about gravity. Mind your own chest. For some reason, my lack of support for support makes people really nervous. I think that there is something about bralessness that is too free, too overtly sexual, too bawdy, too loose, so that it makes people stammer and stare. It isn't my intention to be any of these things, nor do I care if that's what people think I'm doing. I'm not a dancer with a bony seat and no balcony, not one of those boyish girls who can "get away" with not wearing a bra because they're not guilty of fleshy "excess," and I'm neither ashamed nor judgmental about the aforementioned excess, considering it less an excess and more an extravagance of nature, something to be celebrated rather than hidden. My lawless, braless ways are rather outlaw.

But I'm here to talk about the Queen. Her reduction simply does not make her less of an icon in my eyes. The sequence in *Chicago* thrills me, forces me to play and replay it several times a day on my computer, the amber-beaded dress fringes out into an ecstatic aura, casting her in a beautiful golden light. Ostrich feathers and jeweled headdresses were made for that shit, and Bessie Smith is reborn better and more bad-ass beautiful than ever. She made that film truly brilliant, and it became my guiltiest cinematic pleasure of the year, since I just can't seem to get enough of the Queen, or that adorable shapeshifter, Renée Zellweger.

My favorite Queen Latifah performance has to be her gritty tour de force as hard-core gangsta bankrobber-ladykiller in the exhilarating early '90s noir *Set It Off*. The Queen goes down in a blaze of glory rivaled only by Al Pacino's momentous bullet-ridden farewell in *Scarface*. I'm not sure why *Set It Off* doesn't have the same cult following in the hip-hop community as Brian De Palma's epic of a Cuban immigrant with balls of steel and a strangely ethical manner of doing business as a high-stakes drug dealer. First of all, the people in *Scarface* are all in brownface. The performances are brilliant, but, then again, everybody looks really orange. Even if there are a few real Latinos sprinkled in the mix, they fade into the background, chop and get chopped up with chain saws in the first act, wear fly hats and tight, hot angel white pants that look good when they're running and don't have any lines. And the film is about race! I get the heroic thug that Tony Montana is, and am madly in love with him, because he is a gangsta through and through. He believes in himself, and he isn't held back by race (even though it's just self-tanner, but Pacino is a dope actor so he can do anything, really), nor does he believe that his class is something that is going to be difficult to overcome. Like the Queen, he is the true King, anointed not by white society but by his own focus, pride, love, genius, bravery, and some bizarre familial dysfunction that is at once terrifically sad, in his rejection by his mother, and his creepy obsession with his sister. Rappers spend major bank on memorabilia from the film, and there are numerous mentions in legendary rap songs, like when Biggie says, "Don't get high on your own supply."

The true tragedy behind the Jacobean drama of *Scarface* is that no matter how much money Montana makes, no matter how palatial his estate is—Versace to the nth degree—no matter how white and distant Michelle Pfeiffer is as a wife, he will never break through that glass ceiling to the truly elite society that he half despises yet longs for, because he is not "legit." His money is dirty, a veiled allusion to his race (okay, I won't go there again, Pacino is the shit), and therefore his royalty is ignored by the playa-hatin', wack royalty, represented by the blue-haired socialites who cower at Montana's meltdown at the fancy restaurant near the end of the film. The King ends up alone in his ridiculous bathtub, too large to fill without the water getting cold, and self-destructs in cinematic seconds due to his own drug-induced paranoia. He has done himself in through a process of internalized denial of his own worth, a ticking time bomb set off by the race and class values of '80s America. He would be the only one strong enough to bring himself down, and so he does. Even though it seems as if he's the victim of numerous hit men outside his bedroom door, it's really that he cashed himself in, that he couldn't truly believe in his own credo: "The world is yours."

My hope for the hip-hop Kings and Queens of our age is that they really can believe that the world is theirs, that there's an unstoppable force within them that goes beyond the hype and the posturing, that the coronation will not be televised. But that doesn't mean anyone's about to abdicate, y'all.

kevyn aucoin

New York reminds me so much of you. Coming into town, I would always stare out the window of the cab, looking at the streets, loving them, knowing you were here, wondering what you were doing that moment. Then I would recall the smell of lemons, that perfume you gave me last time I saw you, before you died.

I wish you were still here, because the new Patty Griffin album is beautiful, especially the song, "Top of the World." Listening to it makes me miss you, and I can't stop thinking about whether you get the latest music in heaven. Does it drift up to meet you? Do you hear it? Maybe you even get it before it comes out. Maybe God gives you a heads-up, like when Patty was writing the song, and you got to hear it come right out of her that first time.

Tori Amos has two more records out, and they are amazing. She was your favorite, I know, and she loved you. She covered "Rattlesnakes," which is my favorite Lloyd Cole song, and it makes me cry hard, because your life wasn't long enough for you to hear it, but I'm just hanging on to the hope that iTunes are available up above, and the afterlife is rife with iPods. What's on your playlist?

You loved women more than most men, or even women, and you were such a good uncle to your niece. You were forever concerned about her transition to womanhood, whether she would make it in the harsh world of today. You would have been excited because in D.C. there were a million women marching for their right to reproductive choice. The press said that it was just a few hundred thousand, but we are many millions, and because women are everywhere all the time and we were all there. All the many women you loved, all around me. It was funny being surrounded by women while all the time I had you, this big, tall, handsome man, on my mind.

You had done wondrous things with all of their faces; their beauty reflected your beauty. That was what you did here on earth. As passionately as people make love, you made beauty, and not just with the powder and rouge and lipsticks but with your faith, your joy, your understanding. It wasn't makeup, it was love, and that was clear.

Can you see me? I am beautiful, which I never thought was true, but you made me see it, and then that insight faded away, but now I see it again, I can't get away from it. Thank you for that. The women at the march were beautiful because they were there, and they were all focused on one thing: the right to be themselves.

I got into it with a Mennonite, but, you know, I'm straight-up thug, and you can't take me anywhere but Knuckletown. I said, "Step up, come on. Bring it!!!!! Ezekiel!!!!!" He was making his wife and kids hold up blown-up pictures of fetuses that had been torn up, all bloody. Does Kinko's let them print up that shit? I know I shouldn't get physical, but it was early in the morning and I was ready to roll and the counterprotesters made me mad. They're small and insignificant, and the pain is small yet consistent, like a mosquito bite, and if you scratch it it will bleed. So I'm a little bloody but still looking good, thanks to you, thanks to me, thanks to womanhood. It was the largest march on Washington in history, and I wore heels.

Late in the afternoon, I saw Air Force One in the sky, flying low, really ominously, over the protesters, the biggest mosquito of all. I'm not sure what the president was trying to say, maybe that some bugs are never going to get slapped or zapped. There's no no-pest strip sticky enough to catch that shit. Police cars swirled all over the ground, surrounding the crowd, lights and sirens going full blast. Did you see any of that?

Are there lots of soldiers up in heaven? Are they cute? Is it fun? I hope so, because I know that their last few days here on earth weren't. I was just missing you. I always do.

ann coulter

People get so pissed off at Ann Coulter. I hadn't seen her before, but when her name is mentioned in my circles muthafuckas go off. I realized I needed to do some research. Generally, I'll read anything and agree somewhat with anybody, even extreme or stupid points of view, because anyone who can get it together to write a book is kind of cool. And the worse the author is, the more I enjoy it. It never fails to capture me in a web of desire. I got that "You got me at 'Hello'" feeling when reading the foreword for *Slander,* written by high-ass junkie pill popper Rush Limbaugh. I can't believe he was able to put sentences together while on all those fucking drugs, which explains his chaotic and disturbing point of view, and therefore makes him an incredible idiot savant.

I dove into Ann's writing, which was a cross between bizarre accusations about liberal politicians and psychobabble hyperbolic lies that make no sense. The conservative men love her because she is a loyal slave to the status quo. She is Cunta Kinte. As well as betraying her gender, as a notoriously antifeminist woman hater, she is also racist, homophobic, without compassion, inhumane, arrogant, dishonest, contradictory, not funny, has an arguing technique that compares closely to "I know you are but what am I?," wears red leather mini-skirts and is just plain fucking wrong. I can't even quote her because everything she says is too awful for me to write.

All this and she isn't even hot. If you're going to be wrong, at least be hot. I'm guilty of some of the biases that Ann has, only in reverse. My prejudice against and hatred of the establishment, the judicial system, antiabortionists, racism, misogyny, the joining together of church and state can have me spiraling downward out of control, and maybe my facts could be discounted and I could be called a liar as well. But I don't give a shit, because at least I'm hot. I know, I may not be pretty in the traditional way, but playas line up around the block to make some time with me, even when they aren't getting it right then and there. The line is just for the wristband, yo. The hotness is not about age, looks, body type, race; it's about honesty, knowing who you are and being who you are, without trying to front yourself as being better than you really are. It's about the down-deep authenticity of self, then looking it, living it, loving it.

If Ann were hot, then I could excuse some of her behavior. She only goes to the safe end of her sex appeal, ever so slightly flossing a North Beach leather mini with her long legs and crazy anorexic body. If she had some integrity, she would go get some straight-up phat silicone titties, and part her blond hair in the middle, take a pair of Velcro rollers and make those stripper forehead curls that make the boys say, "Whassup, Shorty!!" If she had blonder, bigger hair, that certainly would add credibility to her conservative politics and her upper-class, robotic bigot never-had-any-shit-come-down-on-me-like-a-hard-rain-so-why-should-I-care-about-anyone-but-me values. She can't spit her ignorant angry rhymes successfully with that beige lawyer lipstick. Ann needs to get some Revlon Cherries in the Snow, the ho's lipstick of choice. She's a ho in sheep's clothing, and it's about time she told the truth, the ho truth, and nothing but the truth.

There's nothing wrong with docking cock for the things you believe in, but don't play the thinking man's bombshell with me. Because Ann doesn't think, and she's nowhere near being the bomb, I just wish that she'd detonate and explode. But the only way that she could blow up is to face the '70s porn movie dick-sucking Muzak and own up to her politico prostitution. I'm a ho for the people and I love that, and I'm proud because I embrace my ho side and never try to pretend like I know everything about everything because I don't. I don't have to front because I actually care about people. I believe in equality for everyone. All I ask for is that. But that's not possible in the America we live in today for a million reasons, Ann being one of them. She won't put 'em on the glass, so she's not qualified to throw stones.

bill o'reilly

I hope that karma really does exist. Sometimes I believe that it does, especially in the case of Bill O'Reilly. The sex harassment suit against O'Reilly and FOX News is the ultimate liberal Schadenfreude, delighting in the misfortune of others. I often wonder why there is no equivalent term in English. There should be, considering it's a great American pastime.

I don't fault O'Reilly for being a nasty man. I have no business pointing fingers, considering how many fingers have been in me. If I got slapped with a $60 million lawsuit every time I tried to lay a falafel on somebody, I don't know where I'd be but I'm sure it would involve washing dishes.

Many are shocked at the dollar amount. They say that because the figure is so high, the case is all about extortion. I don't think that $60 million is nearly enough, because a woman's sense of safety, sexual and otherwise, is far more valuable than that, and is something that can never be replaced or paid back.

There is no real retribution for transgressive acts, just whatever the justice system metes out. Consider that $60 million is not only consolation for having had to deal with this upsetting situation where Bill O'Reilly is calling you up at all hours and ejaculating, then afterward talking about how good he was on the *Tonight* show with Jay Leno, but also the absolute invasion of privacy involved in filing suit against the media monolith FOX. Look at the alleged rape victim in the Kobe Bryant case. Even though her identity was to be kept secret from the public, every lurid fact of her life was documented in the tabloid pages. To come out and accuse a cultural lightning rod like Bill O'Reilly is tantamount to social suicide.

Andrea Mackriss, O'Reilly's accuser, became a household name, just like Monica Lewinsky. No matter how progressive we would like to think we are, we forever blame the victim, forcing them into a life of infamy where they design handbags and endure jokes about dress stains for the rest of their lives. Sixty million dollars doesn't even begin to cover it. For the rest of us, it's an expensive laugh charged against the account of one who can't possibly afford it. Bill O'Reilly will never lose his job, or his reputation. He might spin it, how a regular Joe like him can be victimized by a crazy broad, weaving it carefully into the FOX mythology of hate, a cautionary tale about the hysteria and greed of women.

What I find truly sinister about the whole mess is the way that he said, "If a woman ever breathed a word I'll make her pay so dearly she'd wish that she'd never been born." That is intolerable, and what I find truly evil. When we act irresponsibly, we must be willing to be accountable for it, or at least hope to get away with it without people finding out about it, and certainly without threatening the victim into silence. The proper course of action would have been for him to keep kissing as much ass as possible, getting Mackriss higher and higher paying jobs, lighting a lot of candles and scanning the night sky for shooting stars.

He also said, "It'd be her word against mine and who are they going to believe? Me or some unstable woman making outrageous accusations." Why would anyone *not* believe her? Would she go to all this trouble to make these accusations, knowing full well the breadth of the FOX empire and the power they have to effectively destroy her life if she wasn't telling the truth, the whole truth and nothing but the truth? Why do we *not* believe hysterical women? Hysterical women are always right. It's brave for Andrea Mackriss to defend herself, and wondrous to have all the details.

I love seeing the other side of Bill O'Reilly. His bravado in the lusty retelling of his sexual adventures, the fond nostalgia he displayed when telling Mackriss about getting a massage in Thailand and show-ing "the little brown woman" his penis and how she was amazed, are human and endearing. I find I can't demonize him as easily as I did when he was just that cantankerous pundit spewing conservative propaganda. His vanity and naughty antics make him sweeter to me.

They cut the bitter taste of his politics and arrogant manner. It's so complex, all that I now feel about Bill. I hate him for his bullying threats, especially the bizarre one about Al Franken, and for how FOX deals with those who might stand in their way. I hate him for refusing to take the blame, thinking that he would never be held accountable, that he could write his own moral code and live without guilt or remorse of any kind just because of his power and fame. Strangely, I love him more now, too, because he is just a man, with desires and fantasies and vulnerabilities. I can identify with him. I have a vibrator, too! He also has to deal with the public scrutiny of his private life, probably not as probing and violating as what his accuser went through but perhaps for him personally unendurable. He comes off as such a brittle guy, and something like this could likely shatter him. He's cracked enough as it is, so this case was like a car bomb blowing up outside the FOX studio, having built up such a Great Wall of Hate among liberals and most other thinking people. Who knows when the whole structure will crash down all around him—his vanity, his cell phone, his vibrator, his passion for exfoliation, his vibrator—and Middle Eastern food scattered and lost in the rubble? I feel for him, but I doubly feel for Andrea Mackriss.

This story makes me think that, indeed, we are all beholden to karma, and payback is a bitch.

the "fuck it" diet

I lost some weight, which set off a strange wave of paranoia among people who think I have either had my stomach stapled or rubber-banded, or that I'm on some freaky raw food diet or whatever.

What happened was, I was fucking sick and tired of dieting and working out. I was fucking sick and tired of my trainer and any type of exercise. I was fucking sick and tired of no carbs. I was fucking sick and tired of eating five to seven small meals a day. I was fucking sick and tired of thinking about food and not thinking about food at the same time. I was fucking sick and tired of buying clothes that were too small for me so I could "thin into them." I went to a nutritionist and lost a lot . . . of money. I never left his office without dropping at least a grand on bullshit. Pills, supplements, shakes, food substitutes, exercise programs. I said: "FUCKING FUCK THIS FUCK IT FUCK IT SERIOUSLY FUCK IT FUCK IT FUCK IT FUCK FUCK FUCK IT!!!!!"

I stopped going to Fred Segal and buying the one thing in the whole store that fit me. I started buying clothes that fucking fit me. I put away all notions of what diets meant to me, what I was supposed to eat and not supposed to eat. I altogether lost the thought process that carried me through my life—my dieting and exercise regimen— and started thinking about the people I loved, hated, tolerated, laughed at, laughed with. There was a lot of time to read. I wanted to watch old movies. I ate a lot of shitty food. I gained some weight, and it was scary. But it didn't really make a difference. Fuck it. Fuck it. Fuck it. I stopped exercising, and I started writing. I played with my dogs. I looked at shit on eBay. I started to eat what I wanted, and kept eating what I wanted. Not a food vacation, not a respite between diets; I just was going to eat eat eat eat eat eat and fucking eat some more.

Then I kind of started to get weirdly thinner. I get it now. Because I don't care about food, and it's there when I want it, I don't think about it and crave it. Since I can have everything, nothing is that important. I don't need to eat a whole cake because I can eat a whole cake every day at every meal if I want, and I don't care. I don't prepare in advance to eat because I might be hungry later and "they" won't have what I want. When I'm hungry, I eat. That's the weird diet in a sentence.

Here's what I usually eat every day. In the morning, I have a bowl of cereal, granola and Life mixed together. If I'm staying at a hotel, I have granola and yogurt, croissants, one chocolate and one regular, and then a large cranberry juice. I drink a lot of water, and a lot of lemonade, regular Coke—no diet anything ever. After that, I usually eat a peanut butter cup or something like that. Then I get to work— writing usually, recording sometimes, interviews, etc. I get hungry again in the early afternoon, and I eat what I think is a good thing at the moment, mac-and-cheese or maybe pizza. I eat as much as I want, but it's usually too rich to eat it all and since I'm not dieting anymore and don't need to cram the forbidden food down before the diet starts up again, I eat as much as I feel good eating and leave the rest. I leave a lot on the plate because I don't need to clean my plate. Why? I don't have to. And the value of not having to finish all my food probably has contributed the most to my healing with food. I used to feel like I needed to eat it all—all and then some—but it actually doesn't feel good to do that. It doesn't taste good either. I can have more food when I'm hungry again. I eat dinner late, usually with friends. I like appetizers. I'll order three or four types, so I can enjoy a variety of edible treats instead of just one entree. If I wanted an entree, I would order more than one. I deserve to eat what I like. I never eat anything that doesn't taste heavenly. I never take anything home. I never eat leftovers. I never eat when I'm not hungry. I never let myself get too hungry. I never deny myself a fucking thing, because I have denied myself enough things for a thousand lifetimes and there is no more denying for me in the way I live. I deserve all the fucking mozzarella sticks, all the chocolate, all the pizza, all the chicken à la king, and I deserve to leave what I don't finish on the plate.

So there you have it. My big secret diet. Love. Love, and the audacity to actually waste food.

belly dance

I was dancing when I was eight,
I was dancing when I was eight.
Is it strange to dance so late?

I think I might have stopped dancing when I was eight years old because my father told me I was fat. After that, you just have a hard time getting yourself off the ground. It was like I put on lead shoes then and didn't take them off for nearly thirty years.

Exercise for me always meant suffering. Punishing my body for not being thin, or for eating too much, or for not eating at all, or for not exercising the day before or not exercising hard enough, or whatever whatever whatever. There was never a lack of reasons to hate myself, to hate my body. I decided to give it all up entirely, all physical activity. I did it out of protest, because I didn't wish to punish myself any longer. I wanted to get out of the prison of my own flesh. Yet complete motionlessness was not the answer either. My limbs began to atrophy. I began having problems with my joints. My wrist would pop and crack after using the computer. My back was caving in on itself. I absolutely had to do something, but what? I knew that yoga would help, but any form of exercise for me was a slippery slope emotionally, a direct route back to the self-loathing I had just extricated myself from. What to do?

The Cairo Carnival was being advertised locally, and my husband and I felt compelled to investigate. We are great lovers of anything from Africa and the Middle East. For us, they are the absolute source of much of the beauty in the world. The history, culture, religion, art, music, literature, food—our mutual appreciation is one of the things that brought us together. It's odd how belly dance escaped us.

The Cairo Carnival is the big belly dance festival in Southern California. We walked into a glitterdome, a wondrous parade of beautiful women, all in sequins and rhinestones, dancing their hearts out. The audience was practically all women. I had this notion that belly dance was strictly for men, like strippers, but I couldn't have been more wrong. There were women of all ages, all shapes and sizes, dancing for each other and having a blast. I've never seen a more accepting environment for women's bodies. It blew my mind. Here, what is considered excess flesh by mainstream Hollywood standards is considered beautiful. In fact, it's better to have some weight on you if you want to shimmy properly. Women were moving their bellies, popping them out, popping them back in. Undulating. I had never seen women celebrate their stomachs before, ever. The stomach had always been a shameful thing for me, the dead giveaway that I was never going to be the ethereal love object, the chic and popular model, the movie star's girlfriend, but merely a fat and unchangeable human being. In ballet class, I was always admonished for not pulling my stomach in tight enough. In the gym, I was screamed at because I could never do enough crunches. I didn't even like to drink water because it made my belly bloat. These are the reasons I just stopped working out. I couldn't take all the dehydration and self-hatred. At the Cairo Carnival, my belly was free. Cairo—a name that conjures up the desert—ironically is the one place I finally felt safe to drink. Drink in the joy of women enjoying their bodies, loving each other and themselves.

I bought a necklace, an unusual one, which hung low in front. It became a belly chain. I loved it, and wore it so much that I decided I needed more chains. The vendor from the carnival agreed to come over and show me what she had left. She showed me all the lovely styles, and she said, "When you dance, you can just wash them off afterward." She thought I was a dancer! I was immensely flattered, and decided that I couldn't just appreciate belly dance from afar anymore. This was some kind of calling. I started taking classes from Princess Farhana, aka Pleasant Gehman. She's beautiful, an incredible dancer, the best teacher and a good friend. After taking her class, women just glow. She helps them to feel really good about themselves. It's a ministry. I dance every day if I can, and I watch lots of others belly dance.

When you go see a belly dance show, if you look around you see that a lot of the women are crying. Tears for a million different reasons. Because they can't believe how beautiful the dancer is; because that beauty is something that is reachable, accessible, not something that is elusive and distant. Because we've all wasted so many years hating ourselves for how we look and not appreciating ourselves for what we can do. Because we've sucked in our stomachs since we were children and now our backs are racked with pain. Because we have criticized our bodies for so long and have only now begun to feel what its like to compliment them. Because we have wasted so many years longing for something that didn't really exist but was sold to us by movies and fashion magazines. Because, for many of us, we could never imagine wearing something that exposes the midriff and now it's all we wear! Because as belly dancers we are never too old, too fat, too ugly, too anything like we are in the real world.

Perhaps I am idealizing, because I am still fairly new at belly dancing, but does it matter? I love it because I love the way it makes me feel; that's all that really matters, isn't it?

see me

The latest trend in South Korea is getting pubic hair transplants. One would think that it would be just the opposite, with salons all over the West serving up specialties like the "Barely Legal," removing all hair from the area to replicate the genitalia of an underage girl, as statutory rape seems to be all the rage; the "Playboy," a very clever strip of hair, like an arrow pointing down to the point of entry; plus a variety of novelty designs that can be pretty much anything you can make a stencil for, from holiday themes—jack-o'-lantern, turkey, Christmas tree, Easter egg—to one's own initials, from various allegiances to sports teams, even the @ symbol. You name it, you got it . . . on your pussy.

I once chose the Barely Legal, not to placate the pedophiles in my life but because I'm rather indecisive, and so if presented with a chart of pubic hair options, I might lose many valuable hours dithering that could be better spent writing or fucking someone with my brand-new bag. I had it done in Provincetown in the summer, where I make my makeshift seaside home, in a cabin in the woods of Truro where my Swiss Family Robinson drag queen relatives reside, the Trappin' Trannies.

The only salon offering the service then had only a male aesthetician, which didn't bother me but which may have been traumatic for him, since he was young, gay and a huge fan of my work. His hands shook as he applied the strips of waxy muslin, digging himself all the way to China, practically, because for some reason I am fur-lined. He sweat, and apologized profusely as he ripped them off, and nervously babbled on and on about the time he had seen me on *Sex and the City*. I'm altogether a fan of the discomfort of waxing the underworld, and the pain, excruciating and unbelievable, makes me very happy, and takes me to a place where songs from the film soundtrack of *Chicago*, such as "Roxie's Suite," could spring forth spontaneously without notice.

"Is everything okay?" he asks. "Do you need me to stop?"

"No, I'm fine. I'm just Roxieeeeeeeeeee . . . Hart."

"That's nice. Could you turn over for me now, please? I've never said that to a woman in my life."

He was very nice. But gossip is sometimes a little too good to keep to oneself, and old gossip does no one any good, and so Provincetown was abuzz the next day.

"Did you see the new film *Notorious*? It's outrageous! She's fabulous!!!"

"Well, you didn't hear it from me, but I have from the most reliable sources that—leaning in—"she has the hairiest asshole!"

Many screams—loud, low, shrill, bass, alto—a veritable impromptu gay men's chorus around the brunch table harmonizes in a cacophony of abject horror and delight.

"Hm. It figures."

The ladies in South Korea ain't havin' it. They want the forest, and the trees. Perhaps they are just tired of combing it over. The Phytovolume just doesn't give it enough . . . body. Who's got the time to get a weave? Besides, it looks *so* fake. The pussy toupee, the merkin, will have your man smirkin', because it is held in place with a comb, which is impossible to explain easily when caught up in the rapture of lovemaking.

"Oh, I just, uh, I got it cut and didn't like it, so I'm wearing a fall until it grows out. Perhaps I should have mentioned it, but in our earlier conversation there never seemed to be an appropriate moment to bring it up . . . uh . . . the opportunity didn't present itself until now. So, there you have it. I'm wearing a piece. Is that a deal breaker?"

Rogaine isn't really effective down there; the vitamin supplements and the Knox gelatin just aren't rendering a crop worth waiting another growing season for—and so it's time for plugs. That's right.

The Hair Club. Sy Sperling, eat your hair out. The surgical procedure doesn't require a hospital stay, just a local anesthetic for your head and your hearth, and, like Robin Hood, the surgeons steal from the rich and give to the poor.

This is very familiar tale for me, for the women of my family, for my Old World posse. In the modern Korean diaspora of today, women are still invisible, so much so that they go out of their way to be noticed, like making themselves so thin through culturally sanctioned anorexia that it is impossible to ignore the disappearance of their bodies. The thinness promotes the invisibility. Girls become smaller and weaker—they shrink—and, ironically, are praised for the resulting dependence on others in order to survive. To please the patriarch-driven status quo, they have become an embarrassingly large and taxing burden, chewing up the scenery with starvation and silence, winding up in hospitals, force-fed directly into their stomachs, because their mouths refuse to open, to eat, to speak, to call attention to oneself, for it's considered highly unladylike. Femininity by any means necessary.

Plastic surgery with an Inquisition-style edge of violence—surely in violation of Amnesty International regulations, but since the unfortunate victims pay for the pleasure themselves these are high crimes that will go unpunished because they are self-inflicted—is practiced daily as a means to invisibility by adhering to the idealized standard of beauty, which, you guessed it, is invisibility: impossible frailty, lack of presence, lack of substance, afraid of challenge, no fight left—these are a few of their favorite things. Skin is pulled back off the skull to grind the jawbone down to reduce identity, the space one burdens others with, the nerve of having a face. Few Korean women are significantly overweight, so liposuction isn't an option, the fat just isn't there to vacuum out. But Botox can be injected right into the muscle, so that the muscle will atrophy, and, for all practical purposes, *die*. The offensive shrinks away.

If only something could be done about the size of bones. They have a bone to pick with those darn bones. I'm sure a new treatment is in the works to remove the entire skin and have that fat skeleton filed down with a deck sander. Blow away the excess, and there you have it, finally, a streamlined skeleton! But not everyone has the time or money to spend on these surgical disappearing acts, so most opt for straight-up starvation.

My cousin, a girl that my aunt wanted to be *so* invisible that she named her Crystal, you could see right through her. It's as if she never existed, because she's never acknowledged and so she's never there. She has two brothers, beautiful and big-eyed, crushily handsome boys that were men already before their teens, for everything that came from their minds, their hearts, their mouths was loudly publicized and celebrated, and so they grew tall like trees with thick trunks and impenetrable bark made of self-assuredness and pride. They are the family's greatest treasures, their claim to middle-class fame. The elder heads a boomingly successful accounting firm in Japan, with an invisible wife and perfect children, the boy growing brighter and stronger every day. I haven't been privy to any information about the girl, but numerous photographs of the boy have been circulating on the

Internet, which I never download because they're always of him, and I know what he looks like. The younger son works in international banking, trading money back and forth, the very thing that turns the earth on its axis—terribly important, if I understand correctly, or if I even gave a shit.

I never even knew my aunt had a daughter because Crystal was less a girl and more a ghost, watching as her family laughed and loved, lived and thrived around her, and she just hovered above, unseen and unheard, merely a cold spot in the middle of a warm room. Crystal lived beneath the family living quarters, on the main floor of their massive modern home in Seoul, less like a family member and more like an indentured servant. She bore no family resemblance, besides the anorexic thinness most of the women of my tribe suffer from, which is odd, since her parents seem the type to have sex for the sole purpose of procreation only, so if my invisible cousin was a "love child" she probably would never have been born at all.

I never saw her bedroom, nor did I ever see inside her heart, since she wasn't supposed to be there. It was all part of the agreement made with the family, with society. Crystal-clear on her invisibility, she remained stealthy for as long as she could. Then, when she started to appear, it was uncontrollable, unstoppable, uncontainable . . . and it wasn't pretty.

There were numerous suicide attempts, too many to mention, but, then, if you aren't there, anyway, who are you killing? Crystal is forty now, no longer a ghost, but considered a ghoul, and she can't be left alone for a second or she'll slit her wrists, plunge a knife into herself, plunge a knife into you, do anything, everything—to show you that she bleeds red, not clear. Her blood is real, as is her insanity, and her unfathomable rage that is the result of the conspiratorial embrace between family and society and the idealized woman that they wanted her to be. She avenges her enforced invisibility with visibility. You can't take your eyes off her. She's all real, all there, and righteously unforgiving. Her family must acknowledge her now; they must pay for ignoring their daughter for so long that they let society dole out the love owed to all children. Keeping their daughter in the red constantly, leaving a bright child without proof of her own existence, an inexplicable poverty of being.

Crystal's revenge is not sweet; it's bitter and awful. She only wanted to be seen, and now she is, but nobody enjoys it. They have tried to cloak the entire family with invisibility, damning their sons' achievements, making their great success null and void. I never hear anything about them these days. It's as if they have disappeared off the face of the earth.

FAMILY VALUES

"a government that would deny
a gay man the right to a bridal
registry is a fascist state."
—notorious c.h.o.

o matter who you are or what you feel about homosexuality—if you are gay, lesbian, transgendered, bisexual, bi-curious, metrosexual, heterosexual, celibate, hermaphrodite, a satyr, a succubus, a fucking human being—and especially if you are a fucking human being, and really want to live in a country where all people are equal—not separate, not "civil-unionized," not lied to about your rights—realize that same sex-marriage will not harm you. It will not make gay people more "gay." It will not make you gay unless you already are. It will not make your children gay unless they already are. It will not change your life in the least, unless you are gay and want to marry your partner. Then it will transform your life, because it will change your status from second-class citizen to first-, where we should be.

I am sickened by the number of people who turned out to vote against gay marriage during the election. It was less that they wanted to vote for Bush and more that they just hated gays so much; having

Bush as a president was worth it if they could be sure of a ban on gay marriage. While it seems hopeless, and at times like an uphill battle in four-inch heels, we can't run away from it. Then we might just fall. Ever tried to run in heels?

If we are not absolutely insistent, unflinching, strident about lifting the ban on same-sex marriage, then we might as well forfeit the Constitution, cross out all the Amendments, knock down the Statue of Liberty (it was a gift from France, anyway—those peace lovers: who needs 'em?), reverse *Roe* v. *Wade,* pretend Stonewall never happened, reinstate Prohibition, deny women the vote, derail the Underground Railroad, bring back slavery, retrieve all the tea bags from Boston Harbor (actually, let them steep—gay marriage is still legal in Massachusetts, for now), give Patrick Henry death instead of liberty (he's fucking dead now, anyway), knock Paul Revere off his horse, realize that George Washington lied, albeit posthumously (besides, all those dudes had slaves anyway), get back on the *Mayflower* and go back to England. The only problem would be, trying to bring the Native Americans back to life and restore their nations that we so cavalierly destroyed in our own pursuit of religious "freedom."

Without the reality of same-sex marriage, there is no freedom. This is not an argument about homosexuality, or God, or what is in the Bible, or what your moral value system is or what you feel is ethical. It is a no-argument zone. No spins here, not in the least. It is about upholding the idea that America is the representation of freedom in the world. That to be an American is to be free. Unless we have same-sex marriage recognized and legalized by every state, then we are not free. We are hypocrites, for we are according freedoms to a certain group in our population while denying those same rights to others. It is discrimination, and that is that.

I have many, many, many gay friends who are raising families, who are struggling to hang on to their kids, who stay home at night holed up with the boxed set of *Sex and the City* because there is nothing else for them out there in the scene anymore. They have grown up and have babies and are living the lives that they have always wanted to live. They are loving each other and that is enough, just like it is enough for countless families all over the world.

Why are they going on and on about the unraveling of the moral fiber of this nation due to the rampant acceptance of homosexuality? Why is this so incredibly scary to these people? How is this worse than our country waging war at the whim of the president and not for any real reason; the military committing atrocities in our name; the constant breach of privacy in the never-ending pseudo–War on Terror; the elevating and lowering of threat levels to keep us in a state of panic so we have no time to actually judge what is going on? How can anyone say that gays and lesbians getting married is worse than that? What is so bad about it? THEY ARE STARTING FAMILIES!!!!!!! So that is their cause for concern?

But the problem isn't actually as simple as homophobic religious beliefs or just plain social conservatism. Republicans as a whole do not have a particular opinion about homosexuality, other than the odd grumbling about not wanting government-funded programs for AIDS education or research. Gays and lesbians don't matter much to the Republican Party, unless they can be used to bait hard-core "Christians" into working for them. Republicans know that there is a massive population of people who would normally be too stupid to vote, and that no one in his or her right mind would want this constituency anyway, except perhaps David Duke. But the GOP will take all the help it can get.

Republicans know that they may not be able to sway anyone with their ideas on domestic and foreign policy, or their views on the economy, but they do know that hatred and bigotry are great motivators. They get the ear of the leaders of these so-called family groups and Christian media watchdogs, and warn them of the impending storm of gay "legitimization," and they get them all riled up by telling them that gays are going to get married and move into their neighborhoods. As if a newly married gay couple would ever choose to live in a trailer park. They get these Bible-thumping, cousin-humping genetic mistakes and pump them up with propaganda and send them into a mullet fantasia of pink triangles and rainbow flags, convinced that their tax dollars will be used to foot the bill for Elton John and George Michael's wedding.

Hatred is a powerful motivator, and these Christian soldiers will fight tooth and nail to "protect" marriage, marching onward under a banner that reads: "You'll get this bouquet when you pry it from my cold, dead fingers." Although the Republican Party doesn't openly endorse prejudice, no one is complaining if it gets more votes.

It really is genius, harnessing hatred in order to further your own political party. We might wish that Democrats would have thought of it first, but even if they had, the plan to introduce prejudice as an enlistment strategy doesn't jibe with the ethical ideals of the party. Compassion really does block the way to power.

What is deeply distressing is the incredible number of people who are vehemently opposed to equality, and the need for them to deny gays rights simply because they cannot bear the thought of gays having rights. It isn't like anyone who is against marriage equality would be directly affected by its existence. Not unless it's the wedding industry, and then they could reserve the right to refuse service anyway. More likely, they would welcome the extra revenue. It is doubtful anyone would turn away cold, hard cash. Greed, remarkably, has no bias. This is evidenced in the way that Republicans will pander to this creepy Christ crowd, and allow the asinine, the atrociously unfit and the morally repugnant to swell their ranks because it means more votes and money for them, and more is where it's at.

But there is an optimistic side to the whole mess. We know how many people hate gays, and want to create laws and legislate against them. We know that they will vote for a president that they may not agree with otherwise, that it is worth the possibility of the destruction of the planet as we know it, that it is worth the superrich getting superricher at the expense of everyone else, so long as Bush will still make sure marriage remains only for straight people. But we don't know how many people hate those homophobes right back. It is an exciting prospect, because there has as yet been no census taken.

There are huge numbers of potential voters who haven't exercised their right because, until now, there has been no pressing need to. Even though there was a tremendous push for liberals to go out and vote, and make sure their votes counted, there were many more who felt hopeless and didn't bother—or that didn't get fired up enough. For them, there may have been no cataclysmic threat looming large enough overhead. What if we are a sleeping giant, alarm set to the nick of time? I hope so. We need ourselves now more than ever. And we can still turn things around . . . there's always hope. We could be Al-Gayda, the sleeper cell you do not want to wake up! I'm more than happy to help set up an Al-Gayda training camp—don't worry, it would offer Pilates.

How do we win the culture war started by the Republican Party's insidious greed and determination to dominate? How do we deal with the fact that many people voted for anti–gay marriage legislation in their state, so that gay marriage would not only be outlawed on the federal level but on the state level as well? It's the political equivalent of always wearing a tampon and a pad. How do we come to grips with the tremendous amount of hatred and homophobia that exists just beneath the surface of American politics? I think it might be better to look at it positively. How can we possibly lose? Just because legislation passes doesn't mean it can't be reversed. Just because people are dumb doesn't mean that there are more that are even dumber.

The point is, we should not be accommodating this sheer stupidity. The current liberal stance is a backward version of "taking the high road" that ignores the demoralizing and homophobic view of the

Christian right, when, in truth, it is not the high road but what is incorrectly perceived as the safe road. Playing it safe isn't productive for anyone, because safety requires that gay and lesbian Americans be invisible, and the inhumanity engendered by making people invisible is anything but safe; rather, it puts us all in danger. When we are banned from the places where we should be welcomed, where we should not only be allowed but encouraged to speak, where do we go then?

Democrats put a lot of the blame on gay and lesbian consituents for costing them the election over the issue of gay marriage. Yet how can we allow homophobia to be written into the Constitution? The blame should be placed where the blame is due, on the ignorance and intolerance of American voters. Trying to fault gays and lesbians for standing up for their rights is backward and unconscionable.

It is time to hold fast to our beliefs, to create new standards for our elected officials, to continue to commit our acts of civil disobedience.

If gay and lesbian couples continue to line up at city halls all over the nation demanding marriage licenses; if, one by one, the mayors decide to let the people have what rightly belongs to them; if the media sees these families, solid and loving, so many already in place for years and years yet without acknowledgment from government agencies and society at large, if they are unable to ignore the numbers of us willing to fight for what we believe in, if we can become an army of lovers, how can we lose this war? Would they bring out the riot police? Throw tear gas grenades instead of bridal bouquets into the waiting bridesmaids' hands? Hose the newlyweds off the street? "The harder they come/The harder they fall/One and all."

We have no idea how powerful we actually are. We were never considered part of the general, "respectable" population. This land is your land, but this land isn't my land—that is what so many of us thought. This second-class citizenship has sunk in so deeply that we have barely any awareness of it. We had no idea that this is the enemy we are truly fighting. "The enemy is within/Don't confuse me with him." Elliott Smith wrote that lyric, and it feels overwhelmingly appropriate.

That silent complicity with the status quo, even with the great strides in GLBT activism, and the burgeoning, mainstream gay icons on *Will & Grace* and *Queer Eye for the Straight Guy,* has kept the true face of who we are quietly hidden. We don't know how far our reach extends. We don't know our own strength. We don't know that we are warriors.

We are being called up, like the draft, to serve our country. The good news is, it isn't overseas, and it's a war we believe in. It's a war for everything we are. Not as gay and lesbian Americans, but as Americans.

Most voters who vote against gay marriage are likely not to know what they are voting against because they have no experience with gay culture and are just going with the prejudicial flow. If they are not given a chance to change, the opportunity to face the very person who would be negatively affected by their vote, they always will choose the evil they know. So the National Gay and Lesbian Task Force, for instance, makes it their job to go door to door and introduce themselves. "Hi, my name is Todd. I am gay, and I am an American. Let's talk about marriage equality." This type of grassroots activism has helped them keep antigay legislation at bay. It is the simple act of humanizing the struggle, in the most poignant terms, putting a face to a name. When you put your handshake and smile in the brutal face of bigotry, the grimace has to go. There just isn't room in the heart for it.

People might think you are insane, or, worse, a Jehovah's Witness. Who wants to be associated with that Avon lady/Girl Scout cookie religion? Yet the interaction is powerful. It is very difficult to be mean to someone to their face. It isn't human nature. I can't do it with any degree of comfort at all. My spine gets tingly, my face starts to twitch. I get completely flushed red with anxiety. If I have to be mean, I have to practice beforehand. If we take the human kindness factor and use it to our advantage in the struggle for marriage equality, then it will ultimately be what helps us win. Imagine, they will be thinking of you at the polls, worried that if marriage equality doesn't pass you will be back, and, worse, they will think it's their fault, and be afraid that you think it's their fault, too.

Whatever you do to start assisting the war effort, whether it's going to the house next door to tell them you would like to get married, or making donations to those organizations that are fighting for gay rights, or telling everyone you know everything you know about marriage equality, or organizing a letter-writing campaign, or having a bake sale . . . If we want to win, we have to get really low-fi, analog, hands-on. It has come to this.

If you are not gay, it is still your issue, because if we lose this battle who will be there to defend your rights? If the government is allowed to take freedoms away from a certain group of people, how much longer will it be until they come for you?

We are a much more formidable opponent than anyone would have guessed. We've never had a chance to grab the brass wedding ring, the symbol of equality, the real civil union—not between us, in place of marriage—but the union we have with the rest of the citizens of this nation. How strong is your grip?

All we need now is a Martin Luther Queen. Please stand up. Now, at this very moment. This is the most important thing we could ask for. Someone who could say "Free at last" would be nice, but right now I would settle for "Here at last."

In the immortal words of Bette Davis, as Margo in *All About Eve*: "Fasten your seat belts. It's going to be a bumpy night."

thank you, gavin newsom

It is revolting that the gay marriages in San Francisco are being annulled. I don't understand why these arrogant, nosy, busybody, bigoted "conservatives" have to trample civil rights in order to have everyone understand that they think that homosexuality is wrong.

You know what? I think that intolerance is wrong. I think that having no compassion is wrong. I think that meddling in people's lives, people you don't even know, is wrong.

I think that these people who claim to do God's work are actually working for the other guy. Satan likes it when people are motivated by their own prejudice. The Horned One gets all happy when someone is being oppressed or unduly punished. The Dark Lord loves injustice. These so-called family advocates and Christian groups are really doing the devil's work. I hope they enjoy being his pawns.

The true face of evil is the need to control others. It doesn't matter that you think it might be for their own good or salvation. We will see who goes to hell.

I was so proud of my home town for legalizing gay marriage, sending gays and lesbians to the City by the Bay, this city built on rock 'n' roll, to tie the knot. Who doesn't like that?

Well, the bullshit "Family Values" groups didn't think it was right. One dude even said that the new mayor, Gavin Newsom, who lifted the ban on same-sex marriage outright, talking about how "separate but equal" don't play no more, was a dictator because he was changing the laws without any adherence to the status quo and the laws currently in effect in other cities and states. I think the dictator is the one who would keep telling consenting adults what to do with their lives. The one goose-stepping is the one who would dictate who you should love and who you should not love. When you point your finger at me, you got three pointing back at you—see?

The first couple to be wed were quietly exchanging vows in a city supervisor's office in a lovely ceremony. These two women had been together for over fifty years and never expected to see same-sex marriage legalized in their lifetimes.

I am of the opinion that such marriages only enforce and ground the idea of family values. By allowing and legitimizing different types of families, we make them relevant, attainable and honorable, thereby strengthening the moral fabric of the nation and making the ideal American family setting available to all who wish to be a part of one. We will never again have a shortage of parents like we do now. We instead will have a surplus of love and caring, which we do not have now. "Separate but equal" doesn't mean anything when we do not have equal rights. As soon as we do, the world will start to feel like a better place to live because freedom will begin to reign.

What role should gender play in legalized marriage? None. We hold the keys to gender in our minds and hearts, not in our bodies. How does gender identification involve or diffuse or somehow detract from one's partnering or parenting skills? It doesn't.

People should not attach morality to this issue. Morality is up to the individual and should not be legislated. If we were to push our morality on the present State of the Union, it would be an outrage. Go ahead, try to establish a dress code at a monster truck rally. You risk getting burned at the stake like a witch. But then, moral police are already allowed to impose their code of ethics upon our families, or erstwhile families. The fact that this subject is even on the table, that we are openly debating the right to marry someone of the same sex, to me is an outrage, a grievous display of prejudice, homophobia and the power of the church reaching out of bounds, beyond the state. If we were truly following the mandates of the Bible, then there would be laws against same-sex marriage, but not against polygamy or slavery. In addition, there would be no mixed fabrics (not a bad thing; we could all live without cotton/polyester blend), no theory of evolution, but constant burning bushes and ongoing human sacrifices.

The laws and mandates of a nation made up of many different types of people who worship in innumerable ways should not be based on biblical text. That we are "one nation under God" is a fallacious statement that is interpreted too literally, one that is conveniently pointed to as the be-all and end-all to all of this controversy. We are many nations under many gods, and sometimes we don't even have a god, but that doesn't exclude us from being part of the melting pot.

So to all the couples who celebrated their nuptials in my lovely San Francisco, mazeltov. Blessings to all of you. I believe in love. I believe in you. Marriage is not an act of civil disobedience. It is an act of love.

dear governor schwarzenegger

Dear Gov. Schwarzenegger,
Hello there, Governor.

I am responding to your comments on a recent *Meet the Press* where you said if they did not put a stop to same-sex marriage in San Francisco, something to the effect of "the next thing you know there will be riots and injured and dead people in the streets." I don't believe these were your exact words, but that is good enough. Is that a threat? Are you going to go down there yourself and turn that red light on in your eye and use all your terminating morphing mercury ways to stop it? Have you come back from the future to stop same-sex marriage?

Why do you believe that this will have to turn violent? What is so wrong that you actually believe that there will be blood in the streets if Mayor Newsom doesn't stop issuing marriage licenses? Are all the roles you have played on-screen starting to become indistinguishable from real life? Have you played politician before? This isn't the movies. This is real life, and there is no stunt double and no script and no director, and you are not acting. This is love. This is happening. And you cannot stop people from loving each other. What is going on is beautiful. Don't you think that it will be peaceful and joyous if you just let it be? What are you protecting us from? Heterosexuality? Homosexuality? Bigotry? Prejudice? Homophobia? Heterophobia? Flying bouquets of flowers? Rice thrown about willy-nilly? "Here Comes the Bride" changing to "Here Comes Gay Pride"? What effect does this have on you, other than that it inflames your own prejudice and beliefs that gays and lesbians should not have the same rights as all other Americans?

So far, your decisions as governor have not made a good impression. I wrote you an impassioned letter about Kevin Cooper's imminent and wrongful execution, pleading that you not kill an innocent man, and I received a form letter telling me to read some tourist book about our great state. Cooper was given a last-minute reprieve, and his case was reopened, but that was not your doing. I understand. You were probably busy working out. How much do you bench-press these days? I bet a lot. Yet the weight of the state just kind of rolls off your big shoulders, because I haven't seen you do anything except agree with the right-wing conservatives who have nothing to gain in the war for same-sex marriage except the satisfaction of knowing that they can control the citizens of our nation and impede their freedom.

Is it that immoral to you that there is love between consenting adults that has nothing to do with bigamy, bestiality, incest or any of the other perversions the theocrats love to fantasize about— that will defy the status quo? Are you really afraid that this will open the floodgates of faggotry in the USA? Suddenly, the state will start to resemble Berlin in the early '30s? It will be the Weimar Republic all over again, and we might—God forbid—experience a renaissance of art and culture and tolerance. Can I play Sally Bowles? Perhaps the idyll didn't last for them, but it wasn't because there was a "religious right" there to stop the "madness" of freedom and acceptance, it was Hitler. But I don't have to tell you about that, do I? You know a lot about him. A little more than most people do, I would say. But I am not here to judge your role models. It just concerns me when you try to emulate them. He really hated homosexuals.

Don't pretend like you aren't good friends with lots of gay people. If you are an actor in Hollywood, there is no way to avoid it. All the hours you have clocked in makeup trailers in the last several years and you still think there is something wrong with homosexuality? Wow, did you have to grit your teeth every time a brush crossed your cheek? You must have TMJ.

I don't think that you hate gays. If you did, you would have looked really bad on-screen. What are you trying to appear like now? Is this image upgrade going to help the Planet Hollywood chain from dying out completely? Who came up with that horrible Cap'n Crunch chicken dish? In real life, are you the hero or the bad guy?

I actually think the Terminator films are cool. But are you?

Best,

Margaret "Sarah Connor" Cho

i am getting married

I am getting married. I had stopped thinking about it as a possibility for a long time. I got very used to the delicious dream of spinsterhood, independence in solitude, gardening and animal rescue, a varied and lengthy succession of lovers, rejection of the Cinderella fantasies of my peers, looking at settling down like a kind of slow and not all that painful but more just an annoying death, more like a degenerative disease than a stroke. Most of my friends already had a divorce or two under their belts. My fiancé is on his third trip down the aisle.

Marriage for my generation has been a disappointment, for the most part. There is the heady rush of first love, the backlash of the free lovin' swinging '70s key-party antics of our parents, this desire for stability and the pressure to conform. Getting hitched was the emotional part of the American Dream, the pursuit of happiness clause, the completion and reward for the trials of adolescence. The Reagan era gave most of us our values, as we were most impressionable during the reign of Molly Ringwald and the whitewashed vision of John Hughes. The entire Hughes oeuvre maintained that suburban white culture was the true world, the way things really were, how we all wanted them to be. Its power over my generation cannot be ignored or trivialized. Hughes presented to us a tricky nirvana, one in which if you play by the rules you will win—and win big—forever and ever. There were characters written into the thin and uninteresting plots to serve as warnings of the pitfalls in life: individuality, personality, originality, ethnicity. Like eccentric old maid Annie Potts in *Pretty in Pink,* living in the "ethnic" neighborhood Chinatown in order to telegraph her insanity to the viewing audience. She wears thrift store clothes and works at a record store, well beyond her youth, in a futile attempt to deny the inevitable, the fact that she must be married in order to move on, like the unfortunate ghosts of the unjustly murdered and unavenged angry spirits of the dead that must be shown the light, the portal to the other side, so that they might be guided to the afterworld and be released from their bondage here on earth. She warns Molly Ringwald of the dangers of not going to the prom in a cautionary tale about a woman who denied herself the high school ritual, and spends the rest of her days compulsively looking for shoes, keys, subway tokens, finding them all or finding nothing, all the while knowing that she is really lacking nothing, has lost nothing, but that she, for not going along with the traditions and rites of the American teenager, she herself is what is missing. She is incomplete.

In the end, Molly goes to the prom, and Annie Potts puts on a business suit, with a crest sewn onto the breast pocket, and goes on a blind date with an accountant, finally giving in to the "reality" of womanhood, the true purpose of us all. Completion, surrender, giving in and giving up.

In *The Breakfast Club,* Goth-before-her-time Ally Sheedy stops making art out of her own dandruff and allows herself to be made over by Molly Ringwald, capturing the attention of jocky cock Emilio Estevez and finding out that she has beauty, which will eventually, God willing, lead to her "completion." The title song of this film, "Don't You (Forget About Me)," was a sickening premonition of the future, in that we remembered. We remembered to get married. We remembered that having a family was the best thing that could happen. We remembered that we needed to be pretty, and not stand out too much, in order to achieve that final goal: Completeness. Wholeness. Whiteness. Matrimony. Suburbia. Babies. Death.

So why am I getting married? Because somebody I love asked me, and I want to. I know I am already complete, because I've had to fight to realize my completeness, to see it when all I was offered was blindness. I had to force myself to see what was not there. So now that I have seen it, I just want to spend a lot of my parents' money and have an embarrassing semi-Satanic wedding where, instead of wedding vows, we exchange blood. Instead of death, we choose immortality, like vampires. Instead of children, we will have dogs and art.

dear reverend jackson

Dear Rev. Jackson,

I have been a fan of yours for many years. We once shared the stage in San Francisco at Davies Symphony Hall. Your message of equal rights and peace has always resonated with me. Through all the different political and social upheavals over the past decades, you have been a strident voice in our society. I especially appreciate all the work you did to unite the African American and Korean communities during and after the L.A. riots. Your faith was much needed during that very difficult time. Thank you for your activism and your commitment to making our America a better place.

I have spent many years as an activist. I learned from you that people can be encouraged to create change just by listening to someone speaking the truth with love and compassion. Since to me you have always been this kind of truth-teller, I am shocked by your comments at Harvard Law School concerning gay marriage.

This is the first time in my life I believe I have ever disagreed with your views. I was not present, so perhaps your words were taken out of context, but the sentiments were very clear, and as loud as bombs. I don't wish to repeat your sentiments, they frankly are too upsetting for me, and coming from you makes them doubly hard to hear. Your stance against gay marriage is both troubling and startling, and in sharp contrast to everything you have done to raise minority status as well as consciousness in our nation.

I ask you to look back at the many gay and lesbian politicians and activists you have known in your long career. I am sure that many of them might be your friends, or, at the very least, have won your respect as men and women devoted to making this country better for all the people who live within its borders and beyond. Would you say that they were less than human? Would you consider them deserving of fewer rights than other Americans? Do you believe that gay and lesbian Americans are not worthy of love?

If gay marriage is unacceptable in the culture you were born and raised in, does that make all cultural mandates worthy of law? If so, then my marriage is invalid because the person to whom I am married is not Korean and interracial marriage is not accepted in Korean culture. Should we really receive less than other couples who have married within their race? Aren't I obligated to take a stand against my culture in order to uphold not only justice and equality but what my heart would ask me to do? Is it morally wrong to love one another because we do not look like the other married couples we might see on television?

Should we be corrected by society at large and punished by our government by receiving less than fair treatment because we are not white? How is this different if my spouse and I were the same gender? If being gay were a choice, would people actively choose to have less acceptance and more prejudice heaped upon them by society? If race were a choice, wouldn't I choose to be white?

I ask you to review your position on same-sex marriage. If we were a truly free nation, this would be above argument or opposition. As a civil rights leader, shouldn't you choose equality for all Americans?

Respectfully,

Margaret Cho

jobs and economy solution: legalize gay marriage

Every tabloid and even legit magazines had Britney and her "shocking" Vegas nuptials on the cover. My own opinions about Britney and her first marriage were that she was doing the same thing many a young person might do that is impulsive and wrong, regrettable and, well, young, and that we are not focusing on the real problem, her music.

I'm just kidding. I love me my Britney. I'm a slaaaaaave to you. I *own* that DVD. I do not play, and I am not trying to front. Music is my medicine, and I take my St. Joseph chewable aspirin and wash it down with the crunk.

My feeling is that she and Justin really had something good together, and that they will reunite someday. But that is just my own opinion. I do not like to get in people's business about who they want to get with. But they had a CONNECTION that I believe we have not seen the last of.

What people were getting all upset about is the argument that marriage is sacred and therefore must remain heterosexual, and here we have this little girl and her too-big-to-be-that-age man-child looking out onto the Las Vegas neon desert and wanting to do something "crazy," so they decide to tie the knot. Where is the sanctity there? What is so sacred, then, about these kids wanting to escape the boredom of life and taking immediate and not well thought out action to alleviate the dull torpor? Why doesn't the law allow this option for homosexual couples? If marriage is such a holy rite, then why is it available twenty-four hours a day? The ceremony costs two hundred dollars. Some heterosexuals don't spend that much on their nuptials, because since it's so available to them, and so easy to get into and out of, why bother dispensing the cash?

I am proposing something to the right wing who argue until they are gay pride rainbow flag colors in the face that same-sex marriage is an abomination. What I am plainly stating is that if same-sex marriage were allowed in this nation, there would be a tremendous spike in consumer spending, which would ultimately benefit everyone, especially the monied Republicans already trying to protect their fortunes in these financially trying times. Imagine, just the catering alone would pay for tax shelters for the wealthy until kingdom come. All those tiger prawns and bottles of Cristal would bring in outrageous sums. Costly custom tailoring would be the norm, and Vera Wang's phone would never stop ringing. Each call would be a double order. Florists wouldn't be able to keep up with the arrangements. There would be a stargazer lily shortage, leaving frustrated florists to look to peonies and special hybrid roses for innovative and seasonal centerpieces. Wedding planners would become the new power brokers, and Liza, Barbra, Bette, Cher and even Britney could perform at private ceremonies for huge, undisclosed honorariums. Architectural heritage would be preserved, as the historical buildings that lay dormant now would be renovated to create beautiful spaces for weddings, and they would be booked years in advance. It just makes sense. Dollars and cents. This is what Republicans really want anyway, isn't it? Why walk away from financial opportunity just because of your religious beliefs? Besides, nobody ever made a dime off of bigotry. Stocks in prejudice are plummeting faster than anyone can say "dot-com," and I would hate to see you all lose that big money that your daddies left you.

rhea county, tennessee

We need to keep them out of here."

So said Commissioner Fugate, who was trying to make Rhea County in Tennessee essentially gay-free. Queen, please. Guess you are going to have to take *Will & Grace* off the local affiliates, not to mention *Queer Eye for the Straight Guy.* In fact, you probably would have to remove Bravo, HBO, Showtime, PBS, IFC, Sundance, if you want to keep them out of here. Then you have to dismantle all satellite dishes, outlaw all Internet access, television, radio, music, dancing, art, fashion—and you can just forget about Pottery Barn. Abercrombie & Fitch would have to close its doors, as would every theater, nightclub, restaurant, boutique, salon, gift shop, dog groomer, accounting firm, army recruiting office, travel agency, museum, landscaper, hospital, contractor, learning center for the developmentally disabled, school, home for the elderly, church and temple. The entire county would have to relocate, and let only avowed "heterosexual" citizens (assuming this is "us") in after a rigorous and thorough cavity search, and, even then, how could you be sure? There is no real way of knowing, because you cannot keep "them" out of here. You cannot keep them out of anywhere. Because them is you. Them is us.

You have no idea who lives among you, what gayness this way comes. This is like Salem, but this time it's Gaylem. Why are we trying to do a revival of *The Crucible*? Did Goody Proctor witness a man

professing that fuchsia is the color he could absolutely not live without? Did he know that getting manicures *and* pedicures once a month
is proof enough? Is he being burned at the stake? The witch hunts
perpetrated murderous genocide on innocent women, a disgusting
stain on the flag that you weren't ever able to SHOUT out. So why do
you think that this isn't going to leave another mark? Also, if you are
actually remembering that we live in the United States of America,
there is this thing—weird, really, to think about now in this day and
age—it is called freedom. Yeah. This country is supposed to be a free
one. Isn't that a hoot? I know. It was a long time ago, but it still holds
up in court. We are all created equal, and that includes these who you
so ridiculously refer to as "them."

A special message to the guy who needs to come out to his homophobic father: Tell him what is happening in Rhea County. Tell him
that you are being referred to as "them." Ask him if he would consider the boy he raised, his own child, his creation, part of his body,
his life, his everything should be referred to as "them." Ask him if
he would think of you as less than human because you choose to love
someone. Someone who would also be referred to as "them." Ask him
if he understands that you have the ability to love, that was passed
down to you through him, and since he was successful in teaching
those difficult lessons, if it would mean any less if you were loving
a man?

This "them" shit has got to go. I really feel sorry for the population
of Rhea County. Their ignorance, prejudice and hatred is merely a
symptom of the ignancy epidemic that is sweeping the nation. It's

the plague all over again, but this time it's personal. What are they planning to do to rid the community of "them"? Or will they accept them, as long as they stay in the closet, get into false and unfulfilling marriages, have confused and broken families but maintain gender identity consistent with the social expectations of the status quo? Perhaps they would be begrudgingly tolerated if they gave terrific facials, but did wrist exercises to keep them from bothering the locals. Could you imagine if the situation were reversed? "I don't mind heterosexuals as long as they act gay in public."

who's a hypocrite?

I heard about an article that was published in some newspaper that said that Madonna, Megan Mullally and me, being gay icons, are hypocrites because we be married, and that we have no credibility when we talk about how it's wrong that gay marriage isn't acknowledged by the government. I didn't read that shit. I gots mad ADD, for real, though. Plus, I got a reading disability. I'd rather write than read, talk than listen, which keeps me from reading that bullshit. Anyway, even though I don't exactly know what was said, I get the drift. Motherfucker, I told you I was a hypocrite. I don't give a shit. All you were doing was saying, "You know what? You can breathe air." I'm a hypocrite from way back. I took the Hippocratic oath with my fingers crossed. State the obvious, if you want, nobody cares except for you and your mama.

But don't step up to me and say that I'm not able to speak out for the GLBT community, my queer family, to fight for equality for all, to point out the injustice in the world we live in, the demoralizing reality that the people we "voted" into office are telling us we are the same as perverts, bigamists, pedophiles, that I don't have the right to "soldier on" for the cause because I am not gay, because I'm married. I got married so I could *steal* the right that my GLBT brothers and sisters are denied. That's what I am: a gangsta. Why not? Fuck it. I will protest, call for justice, scream out my rage at this travesty, that we must pay taxes in a country that does not count us as human beings, that tells us don't ask, don't tell about our sexuality when we are willing to enlist in an army that would never win anything were it not for lesbians being on our side—and take what is rightly mine in the first place.

I love my husband, but my pager is blowing up with girls that are dying for me to come over and eat their pussy. HOW YOU LIKE ME NOW????!!!!! Ladies like to call me Daddy, and it's not because I had anything to do with their childhood.

I am not Madonna, nor am I Megan Mullally. They are famous, and out of my league. The only person that shit you wrote hurts is me. Madonna is in a different universe, otherworldly and untouchable. Madonna is like God, but she does yoga. Megan Mullally is on TV several times a day and makes more money than I am ever going to see. She and Madonna do an incredible amount for the GLBT community, and their achievements are never going to be diminished by what some newspaper says. Their "Fame! I'm gonna live forever" buys them the power to influence society, and you can thank God (Madonna) for that. But they are celebrities who appear in magazines that don't have me in them, that never have anything about me in them, that think that I'm Lucy Liu, if I get photographed by accident. I am not famous. I just fucking work like a dog, live like everyone else, never have had a bodyguard or a personal shopper. I'm accessible to anyone and everyone. I ride the subway and eat at McDonald's. And I fucking do some work. The stuff I do, calling up gay teenagers to see how they livin', writing trannie kids to help them from feeling alone, hanging with little boys who know they are girls inside and who want to kill themselves, because it's hard to be that way when you live in the here and now—and they just might if they didn't have me around—is not high profile, doesn't attract the paparazzi, because real life isn't pretty, and neither am I. We're not pretty. We're fucking beautiful.

Lumping me with Madonna and Megan just makes me look like a shithead, which I am, but I don't like it when some newspaper says it. Other people can say it, but I don't like it when it comes from an even bigger shithead. Actually, it's sort of a shithead contest, because I don't even know what paper it was in or who wrote it or even what was written, so I think I win at being the biggest shithead of all.

Yeah, I won!

Why do I work intensely for the queer community—protest, demonstrate, endure being called a hypocrite, not give a shit and keep going like the Energizer Bunny?

Because love is love. Love is love. Love is love. Love is love. Mother-fucker.

I have paintings in my bedroom, painted by a man I love more than anyone, a gay man, who depicted the death, the unfathomable loss, the cost of AIDS and homophobia and hatred, the most expensive cruelty, the debt that will never be repaid, the pain stretched out on canvas for all to see, the unbelievable tragedy he endured during the '70s and '80s that he couldn't even talk about, he could only paint it, because if you put words to it, that beat will fuck you up, and you will never dance again. I sleep underneath these works of art, beautiful not only because they are true, they are also born from grief that radiates fresh and hard from them even a quarter of a century later. They are the first things I see when I wake, the last thing I see before I go to sleep. I will never forget what unjust acts I witnessed as a child, against men and women who chose to be themselves. Who chose to love. Who loved. Who fucking loved. Their blood remains indelible, and even though it is not my own fucking personal blood I still feel the pain of the cut. And it hurts. Nobody will know how much it hurts me. A lot. That is all I can say.

I have hate, so much of it in me.

I roll with my girls down the street, with the windows down all the way, blasting Tupac, and I cry my eyes out at the loss of him. He says "faggot" and "bitch" and "ho" and all the shit that is supposed to piss me off, but I don't care because I don't hear that. All I get is his velvety sweet angel voice, now silent, spittin' gorgeous genius rhymes about racism, rage, sadness, the thug life that claimed so many lives of those he loved, and that eventually claimed him—ironically, not by the foes he had in the street but by the forces in the music industry that made him an icon.

I wear a gold pendant on a long chain of the patron saint of border crossing. I respect him and so I do not say his name, I just give him my heart and strength. I am not an immigrant. I was born here, and I don't speak Spanish. But when I think about how these innocent people die of thirst or exposure or police brutality, get killed trying to get over here, who pray to this saint hoping they will live to see America, I bow my head in silence with them. The pendant hangs heavy on my neck, as I try to mentally send those border crossers water, blankets and hope, to protect them from hundreds of miles away. I don't know if that shit works. I just want it to. Sometimes, I think that it does.

I have so much hate that it has turned into love.

What is so wrong with that newspaper article that I didn't read is that it divides a community that is already so divided it needs the division symbol. SHOW YOUR WORK!!!!! You need an extra sheet of paper, fool????!!! This type of journalism and finger pointing is straight-up cannibalism, and it's what's going to keep the right wing powerful. While we ate ourselves from the inside out and rotted like a cancer, Bush prepared for his next term in office. Hadn't he done enough? Weren't we fucked up enough already? Why were we asking for four more years of punishment? So that we can have our spokesperson be "not too hot, not too cold, but just right"? Fuck that Goldilocks shit. And that's not a racist slur. This need of liberals for "specificity" and "political correctness" is going to turn this country into a totalitarian regime. That we offend one another so easily is the worst crime we commit against ourselves. Let it go. Let the bullshit go for now and we'll fight over it later—*after* we win a fucking election. What the fuck is wrong? Fuck it. There are parts of the conservative party that despise the other parts, fucking hate them more than we hate each other, yet they stand together, because they know it is the only way for them to win. The religious right is banded together with groups that sicken one another, that believe everyone but them is going to hell, that carry antibacterial gels with them whenever they have to shake hands, but they are united because they know that the only chance they have to take over the government is if they play Red Rover. Doesn't it make you mad that they are fucking smarter than we are? Doesn't it make you hate so much that it turns into love?

I'm not that smart. I got no attention span, never got an education. I am not real familiar with religion. I've read the Bible, but forgot most of it. Don't know much about, well, knowledge, but I'm sincere. Like Elvis Costello, my aim is true. When I say that we have to learn to love one another, I really believe it. I back my words with my sincerity, my whole heart. If I ever meet you, the person who wrote that fucked-up article that I didn't read, I'm going to hug you, because, no matter what, you are my people and I love you. I might smack you, but I still love you.

WHAT WOULD BOWIE DO?

"strange, there's so much religion in the world, but only enough to make us fight over who is right, not enough to make us love one another."

**lessed are the meek,** for they shall inherit the earth."

So if we play our consensually agreed-upon societal roles, deny our voice and acquiesce to a kind of resigned powerlessness, let the powerful have their way, support the exploitation of our rights and raise no voice in opposition, then we, the meek, shall inherit the world.

Then, by default, since the powers that be no longer have to be concerned with the meek, they can strike out against one another, and violently self-destruct, leaving us with an empty shell of a world, bombed out, like a burned-out house with broken windows about to collapse in on itself. What kind of inheritance is that? It's a pitiful dowry, a worthless and dusty heirloom that nobody wants. What good does it do to inherit the earth when the earth is no longer worth inheriting?

The hotly argued Bible is inconsistent, and Holy Scripture has been invoked in a number of ways to affect the political landscape, co-opting the Word of God as a kind of propaganda. I believe "Blessed are the meek" has been used to silence the voices of the meek, the outsiders, the visionaries, who don't have the strength to come forward with their new ideas. The verse calms the masses; lets them think that since they're meek, they'll indeed inherit the earth, because Jesus told them so; lets them calmly believe that they need do nothing; lets them watch their reality shows in peace.

But I don't believe that is what Jesus meant. The meek will inherit the earth, but not because of their inherent meekness; it's because they've been persecuted and struck down for so long that they've had to defend themselves, they forfeit their meekness and become accidental warriors in the process. The meek are ready to become the new army of the world. And even though they'll be at odds with themselves over not wishing to see blood in the streets, they'll be quick to fight and get it over with, to ensure as few lives as possible are lost. The meek must become the brutal forces they despise in order to inherit what is rightly theirs.

We shall inherit the earth, because the Bible tells us so.

Strange, there's so much religion in the world, but only enough to make us fight over who is right, not enough to make us love one another.

Many years ago, in a galaxy far, far away, my grandfather was converted to Christianity. He decided to open his home to refugee children, and to dedicate his life and everything in it to God. My father's family became like a Pacific Rim version of the DeBolts. Remember them? Remember why they had nineteen children? Because they wanted to help everybody. That's what my family was about. I know that my father truly resented my grandfather for adopting all those kids, and our family reunions are on the unmanageable side.

Christianity was always put to me like that. All of us on earth, like it or not, are a family, and we will treat everyone with the same amount of love and respect. It all sounds sweet and beautiful, but try it sometime, especially when you're waiting in a long line at your friendly neighborhood coffeehouse, desperately needing a Red Eye, with three emotionally charged shots of espresso in it, and the "family member" in front of you is asking for a detailed description of every scone in the glass case, demanding to know which ones have nuts and which ones don't.

My mother converted to Christianity when she met my father, leaving behind a lifetime of Shinto Buddhism. And even though she could "witness" with the best of them, she never lost her ever-loving kindness, compassionate, reincarnatin' ways. This blend of spirituality resulted in a practical, nonjudgmental outlook. It had all the benefits of Christianity, but with a third less fat, and even less sentimentality.

In November 1978, it seemed to many of us in San Francisco that God had died. The Jonestown massacre was followed almost immediately by the assassination of Harvey Milk and George Moscone, and the tragedies fed on each other in a hopeless cycle of despair. I don't think God is dead, just busy. He has the whole world in His hands, so, inevitably, you wind up tucked under His arm, or underneath His chin, and most everyone gets dropped now and again. He has a lot of shit to do!

I believe God exists in everyone and everything, even those people and things that get on my nerves. I see God constantly. I feel Him in my dog's velvet ears. I hear Him in songs by the Dresden Dolls. I feel Him in the throes of deep tissue massage, and really great sex. God rules, because it's all about Him all the time. There are many names for God. He's Jesus, Buddha, Allah, Krishna, Kali, Muhammad, Jehovah, Aphrodite, Ellegua, Shakti, Odin and more. I think all religion is touching, because it represents our need to know who we are, how we are, why we are.

Many of my contemporaries are atheists, and for good reason. God isn't really the problem. Some of His followers are big assholes.

Religion and politics have become intertwined in an incredibly frustrating way. It's inevitable, since both are about what you believe in, and how you live those beliefs daily. I have a great respect for all forms of spirituality, but I feel that a relationship with God is personal, fairly private, and shouldn't necessarily be shared. I also feel that in order to live together in a harmonious way, we have to grant freedom of choice when it comes to worship. Unfortunately, an ugly aspect of most belief systems is getting nonbelievers to go along with you, even if by force. Being a "fisher of men" has become more like a "hunter of men," and I feel that my values are being stalked by right-wing Christians wielding a crossbow just like Ted Nugent.

And now there seems to be no separation of church and state anymore, with right-wing politics becoming more aggressively Christian every day.

But these Christians today don't represent the Christianity I know. I want Jesus to come back and say, "That's not what I meant!" Where's the kindness? Where's the compassion? Where's the charity? All I see are Christian "family" groups wailing on about SpongeBob being gay. They're getting arrested trying to break into Terri Schiavo's hospital room with a box of Krispy Kremes, on their way to bombing an abortion clinic. Where do they get the time? Shouldn't they be preparing for the Rapture? Aren't they supposed to be leaving soon?

Scripture has been left behind, no longer words to live by, just a loose guide to refer to when you feel like it.

They need to read Matthew 6:5, where it says, "Shut the fuck up." (That's the King James Version, by the way.)

passion

I went to the multiplex to see *The Passion of the Christ,* and it was a lovely film. I know how it ends, so it wasn't really suspenseful, but the way that it completely bowls you over is pretty scary. Being raised a born-again Christian and a Buddhist, I always heard a somewhat glossed-over version of the story of the crucifixion. We knew all the details, but Mel Gibson's film brings the whole Jesus experience to new heights. I think his version is by far the most gory cinematic depiction of death to date, and I've spent most of my life trying to shut my eyes in time in horror films.

I like scary movies, but I don't like watching them. Does that make sense? The ugliness of the violence is that it's inescapable. The sound floods the senses, so even if you can't see it with your eyes you can still see it with your ears. The cast in Gibson's movie was remarkable, the costuming brilliant and lavish, the scenery superdusty, the script entirely in Aramaic and Latin, adding a totally different feel than your usual Easter Passion Play, or old favorites like *Jesus Christ Superstar* and *Godspell*. And the camera was unflinchingly steady—and the thrilling turning away of the lens just before the moment of impact is turned on its head and you got it all, complete and bloody.

After having witnessed the full Catholicism of Gibson's retelling, I never want to see it again. This is one DVD that I will not be buying, because I don't want to see the director's cut, the omitted scenes, none of the extras. I especially don't want to see any off-screen antics and bloopers. You know that would just fuck it up.

Catholics are mysterious and exotic to me, never having been to Mass, nor knowing much about it except what I gleaned from Madonna videos. They seem to like to dwell on suffering, what Jesus endured physically, which is so unlike what I always was fed by my Sunday school teachers. My education was filled with acoustic guitar–toting priests with short-sleeved shirts who went on and on about how God loves the little children. In the "Good News" Protestant '70s, we got the singsong fables from the Bible, not the bone-crushing, thorny, nails-in-the-hands-and-feet, splintered-wood Son of God.

The Passion of the Christ includes all the stations of the cross, which are blown up in flashback to Jesus' earlier, prepersecution days, where He tells all His stories and imparts all His advice. It's interesting to learn about the different ways God is worshipped, and how even within Christianity itself there are many different interpretations of what actually happened, and those stories differ in detail even among the books of the Bible, depending on who is telling them.

What I really found compelling in the film is that women are depicted as being closer to God, in very good and gentle relationship with Jesus. He is kind of like a rock star, because he has a hot girlfriend, my very favorite Bible character, Mary Magdalene, and lots of groupies wearing black. He is also a mama's boy. The kind of sweetness that women rarely get treated with in your average Hollywood film is nice to see, even when it's as graphic and tortured as this, with the poor guy always falling on his head right on that crown of thorns. What's really great is that Jesus doesn't ever say that anything is wrong, and He's forever forgiving everybody for everything.

After being in the midst of all this fighting about how same-sex marriage defies the teachings of the Bible, not once in the movie did I think Jesus was being judgmental. Jesus is really all about how we need to love one another, and He says it a bunch of times, not only when He's doing the Sermon on the Mount but just in general. He does get mad at the weird Satan character, who is very beautiful but hairless, a sexy but sexless creature, but He gets mad only once, and that's in the very beginning.

I love it when Jesus gets mad in the Bible, when He is all hollering at people to get out of His father's house, and then when that fruit tree won't bear fruit. Also, there's that time when He yells at the disciples for getting all up in Mary's business when she's trying to put that ointment on His feet. He likes a pedicure, our Lord. So the message of the Messiah, of God and of this film: love everyone, forgive everyone because he or she don't know what he or she's doing, and keep your feet soft.

I bet Jesus is ecstatic about Rosie O'Donnell getting married, because He likes her comedy and admires her parenting skills, but mostly because He loves it when we are loving and happy. To think, He went through all that trouble just so we could love one another. That's why I'm a Christian, and a devout one at that. God and love can't be separated because they are one and the same. The love between my husband and I is what I see as a shining aspect of God, just as the love between the gays and lesbians getting married in San Francisco is God as well. I was stopped at a rally by a man who had been married only two days to his longtime partner. He said, "There really is something about wedded bliss." He didn't finish the sentence, and tears came to his eyes, and then to mine, because his message was very clear. They had glimpsed only the very beginnings of married life, and the taste of it was so deliciously sweet. There can be no wrong here. The way we love can no longer be considered perverse.

Prejudice is perverse. Bigotry is perverse. Hatred is perverse. These abominations will not be tolerated. Love wins all wars; love is all the ammunition you need to fight your holy war. Learning to love my enemies, who are many, is easy when I realize that when I love them the war is won.

semana santa

Semana Santa is Holy Week in Mexico. That was where I was attempting to spend my vacation. I have a hard time relaxing. It was nice to escape to a completely different world, not so far in miles, but impossibly distant from the way we live.

For the important days, my husband and I rattled an ancient rental car up the mountainside to Taxco, a small village famous for its silver and for its remarkable rituals between Good Friday and Easter. The altitude is high in the Taxco Sierra, and the air is thin, as it always seems to be in the rooftops of the world. It's that way in Lhasa, the capital of Tibet, where my dear friends live, two men—one white, one not—who were celebrating their eighteenth year of love that week. And it's that way at the mouth of the Ganges, where worship is the way of life, as if proximity to God were directly related to actual closeness to Him.

Taxco is one of these heavenly locations. It's an evening affair, beginning Maundy Thursday, with penitents walking in the streets, shrouded in pointy-hooded black cloaks with slits for eyes, horsehair belts around their waists and chains around their ankles, dragging bare feet over miles of cobblestone. Old women cautiously walk in front of them, picking up pieces of debris so the penitents won't cut their feet. It's tetanus just waiting to happen, and I get lockjaw even thinking about it. Little girls in white lace wave frankincense burners in the air, and teams of strong young men carry icons of Jesus, all the stations of the cross, heavily on their backs.

There are such cute boys here, about seventeen to twenty-four years old, my demographic, apparently. There aren't many Asian women; actually, I'm the only one. The boys' faces are bright and proud, their brown eyes huge and luminous, and they are all trying to be sly, stealing glances at me, saying "China" to themselves, moving on, but not before I register my dirty, midthirties woman reaction. I kind of wish I'd come alone, but then I remember that this is a religious affair, and I have no intention of helping anyone lose theirs. Besides, my darling husband is taking photographs with all the mad joy of Jimmy Olsen. We share stale pastries and mangoes, and realize that this is our honeymoon, and that nothing could be more romantic. Candles light the night, the Virgin floats above, the choking smoky air tastes of blood. The Passion Play carries on.

Looking up the steep stone causeways, I see a procession of possibly a hundred Jesii or more. Some are most elaborately tricked out, with rims, electric lights and mahogany altars, and they are flanked proudly by countless penitents who are flogging themselves with small ropes with nails embedded into the tips. Other penitents are more lackluster, with cardboard crucifixes and blood that is actually too-orange tempura paint, and they attract fewer other repentant souls.

I'm alarmed at the size of the crowd, and its silence. This supposedly is revelry, yet the late hour and the crowd that by all rights should be drunk and unruly but is not make the quiet oddly ominous, for Christ is to be crucified all over again, and the tension is thick as the crush of the crowd. It's hard to breathe, and everyone feels it. There are few lookie-loo types in the crowd, people who come here to worship, not gawk, and their quiet dignity keeps me from being traumatized by the blood I see dripping down the backs of the pointy-hooded penitents; thorny sticks tied together yoke their necks.

I wonder what it takes to get *that* job. If it's a scary, Shirley Jackson "The Lottery"–type selection process, or if the positions are hotly contested, as to who gets to wear the itchiest horsehair belt, the heaviest load of prickly sticks, who's the holiest of all, kind of like *Catholic Latin American Idol*.

All I know is, this Messiah stuff's really not for me. I'm no James Cavaziel. It looks like it really hurts, and I love God and everything, but there's a point where I must absolutely use a "safe word," even with the Lord Himself.

At times, I welcome pain, and can enjoy many varieties of it, but I said "Yellow!" and He must honor that. I'm a big bottom and everything, but there are limits. Just kidding. Simply put, I'm awestruck by the display of devotion to Christ, and that people believe in a bloody salvation sincerely and absolutely. I, a foreign presence, not unwelcomed yet not asked to participate in any way and have no business at all making light of their faith, nor do I want to minimize what it means to them.

Good Friday is worse. There's an endless parade of hooded men carrying hundred-pound yokes of thorns on their now bare shoulders. They march through the town tirelessly, and there is no end to them. My empathy is taking over. My heart and my feet hurt. I can't take it anymore, but it's become inescapable. Even from the expensively converted mission we have rented overlooking the village, we are inclined to look down from the balcony because, sometimes, even when you want to you can't stop looking. Besides, we can still hear the clatter of the chains without looking.

I want to wash their feet with my hair, ease their bloody wounds with Bactine and clean gauze, put them all to bed. They bring out the Virgin Mary in me. I love them, I love them all. I adore, admire and revere their faith, their endurance, their agonizing love for God. I respect the ritual, the silence, the ancient stoicism that owes much to the native Indian gods that once ruled these mountains, and the people who worshipped them, the mighty Mayans and Aztecs, possibly more than the conquistadors who brought this Version 5.0 of God to the Americas.

The point is, people love the God they love, and they are going to love Him the way they see fit. The spectacle of it is beautiful, poetic, happy, tragic, sad, tremendous and overwhelming, and it shows me, even though I think the Lord is truly phat and all that, that I don't do much for Him. Fuck the Easter bunny. This is the shit.

dog monastery

On a trip to Tibet some years ago, I visited an amazing monastery. Sacred art is commonplace on the rooftop of the world. The air may be thin, but the devotion is given even more weight because of the political oppression heaped upon it.

Everything smells of yak butter, much like the lobby of a multiplex movie theater, because it's used in every aspect of monastic life, from sustenance to tribute. Tea and candles are made from it, elaborately detailed sculptures are carved from it; it's the physical manifestation of God.

We were many miles outside the city of Lhasa. I carried a spray can of air with me everywhere, we could order oxygen from room service. To be short of breath constantly is to understand truly needy desire. Headaches from altitude sickness are debilitating, and we, the sea-level Westerners, took to our beds, or ventured out only briefly to shop, but you couldn't easily buy your air outside the grand hotel so inevitably we returned winded from walking and empty-handed.

When the group was acclimated enough for travel, we hired a driver, Dorje, a quiet, very tanned man who looked like a jack-o'-lantern when he laughed, partly because he was so orange and had so few teeth.

Dorje navigated the unpaved roads up to a tiny village at the fifteen-thousand-foot level. He was incredibly brave, and we sped through the Himalayas at a terrifying clip. I don't remember the name of the place—it was impossible to pronounce—but it had a sinister feel to it. The streets were empty yet the shops were all open, selling plastic women's shoes on row after row of racks set outside, as if the sandals and pumps were alluring enough to pull you into the store.

I walked up the main street to the monastery, which was huge and ornate but covered in dust. I sought it out because the story was that this place was a special monastery for dogs. When wayward monks had been reincarnated and demoted from human life to that of a canine, they were welcome here. There were a few monks who looked after the monastery full-time, but it was the dogs who came there to worship.

Upon entering, I was handed a ball of dough made with flour and yak butter. Gentle dogs, all colors and sizes, slowly rising from meditation, would walk toward me and wait patiently for their offering. I would feed each dog monk a piece of dough, and each would bow in thanks, then retreat and allow the dog behind him to take his piece. Sometimes, a dog would lick my hand in gratitude, but mostly they were more concerned with returning to their individual, private conversations with the divine.

It was quiet, and the grounds around the temple were clean, even though under every awning there was a warm, furry swarm of puppies sleeping against the belly of yet another dog monk. When you walked by, they would look you in the eye, in sincere acknowledgment. "Yes, we are all here. Yes, we are all sharing this moment. Yes, we are all part of the eternal mystery of life." There was no barking, no fighting, no nipping, no chewing up shoes or chasing cars. There were just dogs, of every hue and stripe, with cold, wet noses and sweetly sloping furry faces, sharing the wealth of mystical knowledge with scholars in saffron robes and shaved heads.

These were dogs that did not have the karma of household pets, or strays at the pound, but instead were seekers of ecumenical truth. Even though they were no longer human, they still yearned to know God, and they lived within the walls of this special house built just for them.

pilgrimage

I went to go see David Bowie. Oh, it was sublime.

We missed the opening act but were just in time for "Rebel Rebel." This song is such an anthem, the perfect way to explode onto the stage, and, recalling the video, where he's the glam pirate in the red pants, filmed in kaleidoscopic swirling disco shots of Amsterdam, with his confidently curled lip, poised to hijack the world, I realize I have loved David Bowie for so long because he makes me feel okay that I am myself. I want to wear that same eyepatch and suspenders and long scarf. I long to strut like the dream of the stud that he is, and he makes me feel it's possible. He bounds out onto the stage, and my friend Ava says, "He is just . . . golden." His hair falls anime-like onto his forehead. I want to draw him, although I'm unable to hold a pencil correctly, my warped fingers the reason for that handicap. We can see his glorious face perfectly from our impossibly good seats. There are many exacting and astute words for beauty, and then there is just this kind of ridiculous syrupy, girly idolatry that spews forth, which I wish I could contain but I just can't.

I know big words, good words, impressive words, that is my talent, my gift, my fortune, but I lose them when I talk about Bowie, and lots of people understand, because there is something about him that makes us lose our religion, our intellect, our wit and wisdom, because he is David Bowie, and that explains it all.

The crowd was bundled up against the cold with down vests and sleeping bags. People who attend outdoor events tend to spend a lot of money on Patagonia. The fog rolled in from the beach, and the amphitheater was as chilly as some chardonnay in a box that you'd rather not drink. We were prepared to pay homage to the master yet stay warm at the same time. My friends wore monster white fur coats, and I wore an emperor's gown I'd bought at the Chinese superstore on Broadway in L.A., along with polka-dot plastic hot pants and navy blue kneesocks emblazoned with white stars. To pull it all together, I wore my new belt, made out of real cobra, with the head and long tongue still attached. I'm afraid of it, and I think that it might still be alive, but it looks really good with this outfit so I don't care if it kills me.

The show is incredible, as it always is, as he always is. As an artist, David Bowie has been challenging the cultural definitions of gender, image, identity, sexuality, music, politics, beauty, fashion, fantasy, originality—fucking everything. As an icon, he has been the most inspiring deity to hit the world since the beginning of time. He has no peer. No one compares. No one even comes close. Strangely, he swaggers onstage with a kind of youthful poppy quality that he had less of when he was the orange-haired androgynous fop king in the early '70s. He has grown younger, and a certain humility has overtaken his once formidable presence. It's an acquiescence to age, possibly, a modesty taken on only by the truly great who have nothing to lose in knocking the glossy veneer down a notch to show the truly human being that lives behind the Klaus Nomi confections, the makeup, the legend.

Throughout the set, there are many old classics, which always sound terrific and fresh, like nothing ever heard before or since, and then new songs that challenge his own catalog. It's insane how much of a religious experience a Bowie show can be, the way that he moves, the sound of his voice, his slim, youthful body in possession of the deepest and holiest range—it's a lonely, passionate plea, a sarcastic sneer, a sonic boom—all of it, everything.

There are special treats, like "Under Pressure," a duet with the righteous and luminous Gail Ann Dorsey, whose voice is pure Freddie Mercury, and whose mercurial talent makes the entire hillside shake in reverie. I love Bowie's voice on this song because it pleads with the gods of all things, not only in the lyrics but in the sadness of his soaring, and it makes for a kind of good cop/bad cop diptych: Gail (Freddie) raging to give love one more chance; David, all reasonableness and asking for mercy—this is our last dance, this is ourselves.

And "Quicksand," and the new songs from the *Reality* album, a new favorite being "The Loneliest Guy." It's almost too much to ask for, the ageless, timeless, faultless, flawless Bowie in a vocal storm of versatility, the heartbreaking nihilistic optimism of "Heroes," the fantastic noble androgynous machismo of "Suffragette City"—here, beneath the stars, where I used to love someone a long time ago surrounded by the night sky, and Mars is bright and blinking, like there's life up there.

Then the show is over, and it's time to go backstage.

It takes a few minutes to reach the inner sanctum, but soon we are cordially invited in.

Dawnne and Ava, my dates for the David Bowie show, had a hell of a time trying to get me to stay in the green room. It was scary, and I tried to look for an escape route. Terrified, crying already, trying to jump up on the tables, planning to slide my body out the window, *La Femme Nikita* style, I was there to meet the Great God of Rock, BOWIE—my nowhere-near-false-but-absolutely-real idol. The only wondrous, glorious, prolific, dangerous, legendary, iconic, impossibly beautiful star I had ever wanted/didn't want to meet, because what do you say to God? "Hello? How are you? How's the weather up there?"

Decades ago, when I first discovered Bowie on *Rock Show,* a half-hour venue on Sunday afternoons where they aired "DJ," "Look Back in Anger," "Ashes to Ashes"—before MTV, before music videos entered the landscape of American pop culture—his music made my then terrible world seem survivable. I had bruises on my face from my parents' twenty-year domestic-marital war, where I served the entire time as a POW. Bowie's face seduced me with its asymmetrical perfection. How is it possible to have a face so lovely? Unbloodied, untouched by brutality—or so it seemed to me then.

There may have been sexual feelings, fleeting dreams that involved my lithe yet sensually unaware, undeveloped body. Bowie might be responsible for making me a light sleeper, since I developed the habit then—a girl in a shoddy, sadly sagging, smelly canopy bed—of oddly wanting to be a boy, but in a girly way. These complex thoughts swirled around my head, keeping sleep away, allowing only visions of the future. Was there a way to grow up to be David Bowie yet still be a girl? Would I ever meet him? Would I ever tell him how he shaped my life, my destiny? Would I have the courage to do it if I had the chance?

That little girl grew up well, despite the circumstances. She walks the earth with a heavy confidence, an irrepressible swagger and cadence, due to those nighttime reflections. There were sleepless nights filled with dreams, so many that have come true. I almost expect dreams to come true now. That's what dreams are for.

Today, I can meet the most famous of people. I can do shots of fine vodka with Mikhail Gorbachev; gossip with Hillary Clinton while she gets her mascara done; lie in bed for hours with too-numerous-to-name rock stars; listen to A-listers talk about themselves so much that if you change the subject it's almost as if they disappear, for, without their celebrity, they cease to be interested in you and therefore cease to exist, leaving behind hostility and quiet rage, although their bodies haven't moved an inch.

But David Bowie is more than a celebrity, more than a star, more than an icon, more than anyone, anything, anywhere. Also, he is fucking cool. The coolest guy in the world. There is an intensity in the room that I can't figure out. I'm only trying to get out. I can't meet him. He means too much to me.

As I said, fame doesn't impress me, I've been in the game for two decades. But David Bowie is more than the "famewhatsyourname" of that elegant and eternally loved intergenerational hit song. It is almost embarrassing. I can't explain it, but maybe you would understand if I try.

If you took Beatlemania—the real deal, not the touring show but the insane, truly historical and hysterical Saint Vitus' dance of the teenagers, happening during and around the weeks John, Paul, George and Ringo came to America in 1964—and you boiled all those screams and tears and yearnings of countless girls trying to hide in laundry baskets and under room service carts and made it into a tincture, strong as plutonium, then injected yourself with it, mainlining all that admiration and love and fan club worship and ecclesiastical bliss—but remembering that it wasn't about the Beatles but about David Bowie—not that I don't absolutely love the Beatles, and have had life-changing moments with one or two, but I'll tell that story another time—then you might get an idea of how much of a freak I am about the cat from Japan. If you felt in my veins what I felt right then, you would understand. You would make that the moment you would want to capture and hold in your heart forever, over the river, over the rainbow, into all of your next lifetimes, into heaven itself. Your future self would wake from dreams of this moment not knowing why, but forever and ever replaying itself into infinity.

David is looking at me, and smiling, stealing looks out of the corner of his eye. He is stunning. His beauty is relentless and alarming. Fresh from the concert hall's Byzantine corridors. I wonder if he uses the showers that are always available back there; I never do. I emerge from the bowels of the dressing rooms into the green room, where the fans wait in annoyed anticipation, and they are disappointed, me arriving all sweaty and with makeup running everywhere, friendly, yes, but too small for them to believe that it's actually me. When I meet people, I greet them quickly, so that I might leave quickly, and go to bed. I am no diva. I will sign every autograph I'm asked for, and I love anyone who will wait around to meet me, talk to me, but I can't imagine I'm really all that interesting, especially after hearing me talk about myself for a couple of hours.

But with Bowie, it's a different story. This time, I'm the fan. His biggest fan. My heart will burst out of my chest at any moment. His eyes dart toward me; there are other people to talk to but he keeps looking at me. Smiling. He is magnificent. Time hasn't changed him, not a bit, not at all. Tears are running down my face, and here it is, the moment that I will play over and over again until the day I die.

David reaches out to me with both arms. His hands are warm as he holds my face. He kisses me on both cheeks, and says my name.

He smells like violets.

jerry corsi

Jerry Corsi is one of the astonishingly idiotic authors of the book *Unfit for Command,* that infamous attempt to smear John Kerry's Vietnam military record, claiming he betrayed his fellow soldiers by alleging they committed atrocities while he earned his medals by indiscriminately killing a Viet Cong teenager.

Corsi appears frequently on freerepublic.com, an online right-wing insane asylum, and at one point he had to make a public apology for posting: "Islam is a peaceful religion—just as long as the women are beaten, the boys buggered and the infidels are killed." He said that his words were taken out of context, and he was sorry if he had offended anybody. What context would these statements not be offensive in? A Ku Klux Klan rally? A neo-Nazi music festival? A GOP convention? These types of statements make Jerry Corsi unfit for comment—on anything, really—let alone politics.

I'm constantly amazed how absurdly ignorant some people can be. They act as if they are the only beings on earth. Their reality is terribly knee-jerk, and they have a manner of speaking that reeks of the arrogance of independent thinking even though they possess precious few independent thoughts.

It's depressing how much we'd rather believe what we are told than find out things on our own. We are bombarded with propaganda today that tells us to blindly believe that Islam is bad, that the religion itself is somehow un-American, that evil springs from the Fertile Crescent. If only the world were so simple, that all bad people came in one color so that they could be stamped out effectively for the good of all. Corsi and his ilk—and there are many—believe that this is true, and they're looking for the best way to make it known without meeting too much resistance from anyone who thinks for him- or herself.

Corsi's statement is clumsy and incorrect. Domestic abuse is global. If you pay attention to the latest rumors surfacing about the Iraqi prison scandal, the death tolls on both sides show that the "infidels" are cleaning up, and it seems that American soldiers are doing a lot of the boy buggering.

This whole war is subtly slanted as being between Islam and Christianity, but it isn't. It's about oil and ownership, but since people can't grasp the idea that their government might lie to them, that the people they might vote into office (or, more likely, let cheat their way in) care far more about their own interests than the lives of American soldiers or Iraqi civilians, it's much easier to make it a "holy war." God becomes the ultimate gauntlet to throw down, because no one questions or gets specific with God. God is approached with apprehension, fearful of argument, with bowed head and offering in hand.

When it comes to religion, people are hyperaware, intensely sensitive, incredibly myopic. There is the unstated but implied absolute superiority of the Protestant faith, for to make reference to it would be to cast doubt upon it. There is an air of cleanliness about these denominations, almost a sanitized secular quality, as if they were the only true way to salvation, a path that is so clear it doesn't seem like a path at all. These sects are like Diet God, all the heaven but none of the calories. Other faiths are looked upon with suspicion that borders on justified rage at its most malevolent. Atrocity is easy when you assume your victim is godless. If God sees what we were doing in His name, He must weep copiously indeed. How about that Hurricane Charley?

The apology Jerry Corsi made is questionable, as I can't imagine that he could be really sorry for what he said when he is so flip and arrogant about it. The casual nature of his hatred is evident in his absolute devotion to nonthinking. He's not sorry for what he said; he's sad people called him on it. Because to be a true veteran for truth, you can't be what he is: an adolescent, irresponsible, cowardly, ruthlessly immoral, unfunny bigot.

Here's more of Corsi's genius: "So this is what the last days of the Catholic Church are going to look like. Buggering boys undermines the moral base and the lawyers rip the gold off the Vatican altars. We may get one more pope, when this senile one dies, but that's probably about it."

I'm no huge fan of the pope, but, then again, Corsi claims to be a devout Catholic, so I'm not really sure what that's about. Is he looking to get Bush into the Vatican, too?

And that's not all: "After he married TerRAHsa, didn't John Kerry begin practicing Judaism? He also has paternal grandparents that were Jewish. What religion is John Kerry?"

What's the meaning behind the spelling of Theresa Kerry's name? Is that a way to Arabicize her in order to insult her? If so, then that's a double slur, not only because it's derogatory toward the Arab and the Jewish worlds in assuming that to be part of either is a bad thing, it also makes her out to be some kind of faith bandit, inferring that she would be the one controlling the nation with her wicked, witchy Judaic ways. It's saying the potential First Couple might be Jewish. And why's that such a bad thing? Dreidels in the White House is no cause for alarm. What's so scary about Passover? Who cares what religion they are? It matters less to me that they are religious than that they care. Incidentally, the Kerrys are Catholic, which to the backward, let-other-people-do-their-thinking-for-them-like-it-was-laundry, Charlie Daniels–listening, freerepublic.com-posting, FOX News–watching, Bush-voting, Islam-despising, everyone-who-ain't-us-hating nincompoop contingent is practically an ancient pagan earth religion.

Jerry Corsi immediately rebukes himself with his own prejudice and bigotry. Once you see someone's ignorance, you can't see anything else. It's the glorious thing about stupidity: it's sticky. Those who didn't think that Corsi was a dummy before now have to admit just how dumb he really is. What's dangerous is, the real morons only will see more of themselves in him. And I hope there's more of us than there are of them.

jimmy swaggart

Jimmy Swaggart thinks the idea of one man marrying another man is ludicrous, and announced on TV that he'd never met a man he wanted to marry. Then he threatened to kill any man who gave him the eye, that he would "tell God that he died."

I believe in free speech, and Swaggart has a right to say what he likes, but it's irresponsible, and highly un-Christian, to advocate murdering someone and lying to God about it. His words point to all kinds of crazy. He clearly has a history of insanity, with his odd, well-documented relationship with a prostitute, which caused him to leave his ministry and beg for forgiveness from his congregation. I think the congregation *did* forgive him, out of embarrassment, hoping he would just shut up, if nothing else.

People think too simplistically nowadays. They need only sound bites to sustain them. This is why the news anchors on the FOX network always coin and then repeat catchphrases, to manipulate and brainwash the masses. The ease with which the message is heard and assimilated is the key to FOX's success, and ultimately may lead to the demise of democracy itself. Isn't that sad? That stupidity alone might take America down?

That's what Jimmy Swaggart was aiming at. But isn't it just plain dumb to think that if you killed someone you could hide it from God? That's the scary thing about Swaggart's statement. It would not take much for him to end another man's life, and all he would have to tell God is that the dude just died. What happened to "Thou shalt not kill" or "Thou shalt not bear false witness against thy neighbor"? There's nothing in the Bible that says, "Thou shalt not cruise"!

Why does Jimmy Swaggart get a free ride through sin city? Because God really hates gays too? When did *that* happen? Swaggart should recant his hateful statements, and truly apologize to the gay community. If he did, it would be a miracle. But it's going to take more than a miracle to change the minds of people who believe that homosexuality is wrong.

I have a terrible suspicion that you can't really change these people's minds, that even glaringly obvious logic wouldn't penetrate the hardened heart of one of these false Christians. They're too dumb to fight. They keep bringing God into it, stating and restating what the Bible supposedly tells us, that we are going to hell. They've never really read God's Word; they just know the slogans. Christianity took a wrong turn somewhere.

There are major problems with the way prejudice and bigotry are sanctioned by the Church. They are at cross-purposes with the nature of Christ, which is tolerant and compassionate. Since when does the righteous God overshadow the loving God? The only way to solve this Christian-chaos problem is to have a true separation of church and state. Only then can we begin to recover from this ecumenical nightmare, and get back to the business of democracy.

THE RIGHT TO LIFE

"so many people on death row do not belong there. we kill the innocent time and time again. the american judicial system is guilty of more crimes than any criminal . . ."

Here is something you can't understand
How I could just kill a man.

—CYPRESS HILL

I love this song, and, of course, the lyrical mayhem and murdering rhymes of the great Cypress Hill. B-Real's sneery, cheery cadence lends lightness to the incomprehensible idea of taking another's life. But, then again, is taking another's life so incomprehensible? Cypress Hill also speaks to me because I have such rage inside me, because I ask myself, all the time, could I just kill someone? I think we all have that killing instinct, that fire, in us. It is an animalistic yet highly human response. When I am behind someone at a tollbooth and he doesn't have the exact change, I shudder to think what his fate would be if I were packing heat. When I go to the post office, where the lines are always too long, and the window way down at the end is about to close, leaving only one window open out of the dozen that should be open, it reassures me to know there is a seven-day waiting period to purchase a firearm, which inevitably would place me in another long line, so that killing a slow-moving clerk would do no good except to expedite my own death by firing squad. Since I haven't yet picked up a sledgehammer and really brained the last salesgirl who wouldn't let me take more than three items into a dressing room, the death penalty is probably the deterrent it's meant to be, that perhaps we are all afraid to die, scared enough to check ourselves before we wreck ourselves. But I don't know if I'm as afraid of death as I am of jail, and I don't know if I'm as afraid of jail as I am of boredom. A lengthy jail term would be so unbearably boring that a death sentence might be a welcome reprieve. But that's just me.

What is that saying "Judge not, lest ye be judged"? I can't help but judge, and that is why I hate judgment. I dare not cast the first stone because my arms are loaded down heavily with sin rocks. Looking at my own prejudices and biases, which might be different than those of the status quo yet which dwell in my heart nonetheless, I hate to think that I am guilty of the same crime as those whose ideas I try so desperately to fight. If I have the capacity for such hideous thinking, I don't want to know the thoughts of those who might be less compassionate. If I can't trust myself to make life-or-death decisions for people around me—don't get me wrong, I *trust* myself—I certainly don't think that the government should have the power to enforce the death penalty, in any situation. If my own murderous tendencies can rise to the surface, how could I, in good conscience, place the power of life or death in the hands of a bureaucracy? Or, worse, a theocracy?

So many people on death row do not belong there. We kill the innocent time and time again. The American judicial system is guilty of more crimes than any criminal—yet the issue never seems to get anywhere.

The prisons are so racially imbalanced, what could the reason for that be other than clear and present racism? We have special "hip-hop cops"! There are no law enforcement specialists for other "non-ethnicity"-driven music. Could you imagine the "Emo-enforcers"? Narcs in JESUS IS MY HOMIE T-shirts and reddish brown vintage Levi cords, alternating between riding skateboards, hiding in bushes and documenting Conor Oberst's every move? "Okay, he's leaving his girlfriend's house. I believe that the suspect is crying. Copy that. We will be requiring backup. Tell them to bring Kleenex." He is sweet, I love that little white boy, he is very sensitive and deep. But I wouldn't consider him any less dangerous than, say, 50 Cent. It's always those quiet, unassuming types who blow up buildings or spray schoolyards with bullets.

the morning after

The Bush administration blocked the availability of the morning-after pill over the counter, saying that it would promote "promiscuity." I beg to differ. When I was younger, I never had any kind of access to morning-after pills, but that did not stop me from fucking my way through the USA like I was Lewis and Clark.

The "fact" that the morning-after pill may promote promiscuity is the main objection to its availability. I would keep a stash of them under my bathroom sink, just in case, and I'm married. My chances of promiscuity are nil. When you get to a certain age, you become absolutely sick of fucking around. It's sad, but it happens.

But here is the fact. The morning-after pill does not promote promiscuity; it promotes ease in dealing with an unplanned or unwanted pregnancy. Unplanned or unwanted pregnancy does not equal promiscuity. All we are doing by making the morning-after pill readily available over the counter is to provide women with an alternative to having children they did not mean to have, prevent abortions, give more choices to women in need of more choices.

It's simple: There's got to be a morning after. The morning-after pill should be available over the counter, right by the Listermint strips, the Mentos, the toenail clippers, the tabloids—all those impulse buys. I want morning-after pills with my check at dinner. I want morning-after pills on my hotel pillow before I go to bed at night. Reproductive rights are not "rights" that we should need to struggle to get. They should be a given.

And if the problem is promiscuity, then why does the immense popularity of Viagra go unchecked? Doesn't it make more sense to leave the bullets out of the gun than to try to avoid being shot? Especially when the gun is an old musket, and you have to clean it out and tamp down gunpowder, melt down scraps of lead and pour it into a mold, wait for it to cool . . . only to have it take forever to finally go off?

So then are we to assume that the prevailing attitude about women's sexuality is that, if left unchecked, without the possible consequence of pregnancy, women would fuck willy-nilly until everyone is left waiting for a ride home from school or dinner because we are all out trying to hump fire hydrants? Are we in danger of losing half the workforce because we might be generating a huge pussy cyclone, threatening to engulf everything in its path? "Just spotted off the coast of Florida, it's Hurricane Poontang!" Is a vagina without restraint just as good as a vagina gone wild at spring break? Have we no faith in reserve, prudence, common sense, education, social mores, parenting, when women are left to themselves?

This is a political debate. Who argues about choice for women and health care? If it isn't politicians and doctors being lobbied by political groups, then who? If the argument against the morning-after pill is that it poses a danger to underage girls, then why does this have to exclude all other women? Even so, isn't having to have an abortion more of a danger to girls?

Look, I have had an abortion. If I were to use the most polite terms to describe my experience, I would say, "It wasn't a fucking tea party." It is painful and hideous. Everyone leaves in a bad mood, which turns worse. If it could have been prevented by going to the drugstore to pick up some pills, then it wouldn't have ruined my sex life for several months afterward, as I tried to heal the wounds that the surgery had left behind. I would have been able to return to work sooner. I would have been able to feel like I wasn't being punished somehow for the choices that I made regarding my own health and sanity.

We are all women, but we are not all mothers. No matter how much love and respect I have for mothers in general, there are many women who are not cut out for that particular occupation. I, for one, am far too overqualified, and far too grossly unfit. I would be an unre-markable and selfish parent. In fact, I would go as far to say that I would be a ghastly mother.

If there is a safe way to avoid the horrendous methods that we use today to terminate pregnancy, hand it over. Do it now. Before it gets ugly. It's already too ugly to begin with.

plan c

It's absolutely ridiculous to preach to the younger generation that abstinence is the only way to go with sex. At that age, your body is saying just one thing: "This feeling that I have inside is soooo goood, I just wanna do it, here's someone who is gonna do it with me, I don't really get it because everybody's telling me to practice abstinence, but fuck that. So, since we're both in trouble anyway, fuck it. LET'S DO DIS!!!" Preaching abstinence is not right, is not realistic, is just plain stoopid, ignant, duh-duh-duhm.

Remember the young woman who flew to France to get RU-486 and then got right back on the plane and returned to the U.S. only to be greeted by flashbulbs and police? What the fuck is wrong with people? I'm not saying that everyone should fuck themselves insane bonobo style and then throw their shit all over the place, but what's with this puritanical attitude? Like this woman needed a big *A* sewn on her chest to show all that she ABORTED. I want to sew a big *I* for IGNANT on everybody's chest who was involved in putting this woman through fucking hell for having a body and the courage to do what she wanted with it.

Plan B is the morning-after pill that the FDA decided American women could not be trusted with.

What is plan A? Abstinence? And we got rights over everybody and their mama's uterus? Put it in the A-S-S only?

I am not pro-death. I am pro-choice. I am of the mind that young people will find a way to do what they naturally will do without possibly hurting themselves even if we tell them NOT TO DO IT. Young people have strong emotions, intense hormones, that will not be silenced as easily as saying, A-B-S-T-I-N-E-N-C-E. What they need is education, options, condoms, counseling, help, confidence, gentle awareness, trust in teachers, confidentiality, equality, reality, the fucking truth, the whole truth and nothing but the truth so help us all God—not GUILT.

Because ABSTINENCE = GUILT.

Guilt = low self-esteem.

Low self-esteem = everything you're going to get if you offer only abstinence as your only solution.

So if they're going to limit the availability of plan B, then I would like to propose plan C.

C stands for CUNT. Not a curse word, not a slur, not a bad thing. As Inga Muscio's important, brilliant book of the same name, CUNT is the celebration of the woman and the world, as we are one and the same. We would have no world without the CUNT, so anyone who uses this as a negative, transgressive word is denying the fact we are alive. We are all born from cunts. Where we all come from as a human race, our very first home address. No matter where your mail gets forwarded to now, everyone everywhere had this on that first mailbox:

Me, CUNT, the World.

This makes the cunt powerful. And that power includes the power of choice, the power of knowledge, the power of attorney, the power of cunnilingus, the power of veto, the power of everything it wants and DOES NOT WANT, anytime, anywhere, anyway, all the time for all time. For real. That is what I am talking about.

west memphis three

Damien Echols currently is on death row in Arkansas. He has been there for almost eleven years for a crime he did not commit. He is there because of bigotry. Currently, Damien is part of the West Memphis Three, accused of the murder of three little boys, and caught up in the insanity of a community that sentenced him to death and the other two, Jessie Misskelley and Jason Baldwin, to life without parole.

No evidence was ever found to connect the then teenagers to the killings. It was all hysteria over the possibility of a satanic cult thriving in their community, and a complicit court system, which glossed over the facts in order to placate the outrage of the locals, and, to this day, cannot admit what they have done wrong.

One day, three little boys were found dead in a river, their bodies drained of blood and horrifically mutilated. A grief-crazed community looked desperately for a killer in their midst. Most of the clues had been washed away down the river, having first been trampled on by hapless law enforcement officials. Damien, Jason and Jessie were charged with the murders not because there was any kind of proof that they had indeed committed the crime, but because they were loners, outsiders, throwaway kids, and, therefore, convenient scapegoats. They dressed in black and listened to heavy metal, and logic, rationality and justice could not compete with the anger and fear of the small town, the small-minded locals.

There have been two documentaries made about the case, *Paradise Lost* and *Paradise Lost 2: Revelations,* and several books and articles have been written or are in the works. There are Web sites dedicated to the West Memphis Three. And celebrities like Eddie Vedder and Winona Ryder have tried to help. All to no avail. What right does a system that cannot even sufficiently prove their guilt have to their lives? Not only have the terrible crimes gone unpunished, their effect has grown and spread like a cancer in the lives of these three young men and their families.

Of course, there are criminals who have been apprehended and justly jailed for their crimes. I am not asking that prisons and institutions for the criminally insane open their doors, like school is out forever. Still, how can we allow those who do not benefit from the technological advancement that forensic science has made in the last decade to wither behind bars? (I say "we" because unless they are free, none of us are free.) DNA evidence is the real deal, the be-all and end-all when it comes to determining who is lying and who is not. It's better than Wonder Woman's golden lasso. Unfortunately, it's expensive, and therefore mostly unavailable to those who are serving time for crimes they didn't commit years ago. The only reason they probably were incarcerated in the first place is that they couldn't afford to mount a proper defense. But here is a case where we have the most technologically advanced evidence—and it points to wrongful conviction. We have a case where the wrongfully convicted enjoy wide and passionate support and still the government does nothing. What chance does that leave for some poor kid on death row who is not in the media spotlight, who lacks the resources to prove his own innocence?

I have followed the West Memphis Three case for many years. I can't help but identify with their situation. I understand their sense of isolation and exclusion. They are my people, disaffected, disillusioned, disappointed and discarded by the world. I feel for them, and I want to know what else I can do. Recently, I have decided to step up my game. I started by sending Damien books from his Amazon.com wish list. I began to write to him about what life and the world is like out here. I learned that he's bright and gentle, and very apologetic when he falls behind in his correspondence. We write to each other about books, art, spirituality, prison life, married life. We find we are very much alike, just that I'm out here and he's in there.

Then I decided to visit him.

The people in Little Rock are friendly—alarmingly so. The politeness and hospitality there borders on invasive. Everyone is a guest in their state, and you are treated accordingly, lest you forget it. We are welcomed with questions and curious smiles. It is strange, especially coming from Los Angeles, possibly the rudest city in the nation, with a population that is exceedingly unhelpful. Once I was screamed at by the operator manning the 911 switchboard for trying to report a dead body I had seen on the street. Apparently, I was not the first caller, and somehow I should have known that.

But we are in Little Rock to visit Damien Echols, who is incarcerated at the maximum security prison in Grady, an hour outside of the city. Everyone wants to know what we are doing here, why we are doing it, when we are doing it, what we expect to get from doing it and when we think we will be done doing it. Then it's cheery smiles all around, which fade slightly once we get out of earshot.

We have a glorious dinner with Damien's amazing and lovely wife, Lorri Davis. She is a true hero in the face of injustice, and her work inspires me every day. We are meeting with their new lawyer, Theresa, who is doing great work on the case, and with Mara Leveritt, the author of *Devil's Knot,* the definitive book on the West Memphis

Three. We discuss the politics of the case at length, the difficulty of the appeals process, how hard it is to undo the damage that the law itself has brought on due to its own mistakes.

Here is a remarkable trio of women, committed to justice and freedom, who are invested not only on an extremely personal level but on a philosophical level as well. The bottom line of all of this is, you cannot let the government throw people away, because there will always be a fine net of tenderness that prevents it. Humanity is a natural foil for inhumanity, and humanity is what will ultimately keep us going when all else has failed.

A kind of failure is evident when we approach the prison in our rented minivan. It's early in the morning and already approaching 100 degrees, with lung-stopping humidity. The insects congregate in thick clouds near the ground, and they carpet the inside of the car when the doors are cracked open. We pass a large group of inmates, mostly black men, working the field with hoes. They break the ground under the blazing sun and the heated gaze of many Boss Hogg–type guards, on horseback and with rifles at the ready.

We blink several times to accept his reality. It looks like *Roots,* which can never be a good thing. Not then, and certainly not now. I hope that these prisoners have done wrong, that they are being punished fairly, that they are supposed to be here, that their karma has brought them here and not the bureaucratic unfairness of capitalist society. How can we be sure anymore? I have been around so-called criminals, reformed and otherwise, for my entire life. What is common among them is forever claiming innocence, no matter what the accusation is or how much evidence is stacked against them.

Often, it's easy to tell who is guilty and who isn't. Here, it is less obvious. The story of the West Memphis Three makes you question whether any of these young men toiling in the muggy morning heat deserve their lot. Damien once wrote to me that Jessie Misskelley worked the hoe squad and that he felt sorry for him.

We are stopped by the guards on the way in for an extensive search. They filter through Lorene's bag and take out some Balance bars, but not others. They decide to leave my hot-pink Sailor Jerry pocketbook alone, presumably because there is a painting of a naked lady on it. I take my pocketbook back out to the car, since it's too racy for prison, and, who knows, maybe I baked a file in it. I scoop up big handfuls of quarters for the vending machines and carry them around in my sweaty fists. I had been advised by Burk Sauls, who for the last twelve years has been leading the movement to free the WM3, on WM3.org, to bring lots of change for diet Dr Peppers and candy bars. Inmates are allowed these treats only in the visiting area, and they are enormously appreciated. A female guard asks me about my elaborate gold arm bracelets that I wear up high, near my shoulders, like a belly dancer. She wonders if they are "jewelry," and sighs and shakes her head when I tell her yes, like having them on must be some kind of arduous task.

We walk through numerous doors, and then down a long, winding outdoor path. It would be a pretty day, with the cloudless blue sky overhead, if we didn't have to look at it from behind the scary, razor-sharp, electrified barbed-wire fence. You want criminals to live like this if they have hurt you, robbed you, raped you. If they have taken a life, then this is the life they should get in turn. However, this is not what my friends have done.

I hate that my friends live like this.

We are brought to a large, refrigerated building, with glass partitions and steel walls. After the slamming of countless doors, starting in the distance and then coming closer, Damien is finally brought to the other side of the glass. He is hard to hear through the air vents, but he is wonderful to see.

Damien is beautiful like a girl, with a pale, delicate complexion that is Dove Cleansing Bar–worthy. I exclaim that he is one-quarter moisturizing cream, and Lorene says you can see them pouring the cream into the bar, just like in the commercial. Lorri and Lorene both think that he has a Johnny Depp quality, but I think that Damien is much cuter. Though we have never met face-to-face until now, we know each other well, although he's much shyer than I expected him to be. I wonder what he would have been like if he hadn't become a tragic victim of circumstance. He might be living on a houseboat in New Orleans, writing historical novels and giving lectures on the nature of compassion at the local Zen center. He is an inspiring teacher and a remarkable thinker. His writing is a constant source of wonder to me—I genuinely admire it, its quality, its intelligence, its hope, especially now that I've seen the captivity he lives in.

We sit for many hours, which go by much too quickly. He reads his poetry, which is eloquent and dreamlike. I am reminded of Lewis Carroll daguerreotypes, in the fragile, childlike features of his face. He wants me to tell Jason that he would like to find a way that they could communicate, whether it is through other people or relayed messages. Their closeness hasn't faded, even after being separated for over a decade.

When it's time for him to go, it's hard to say good-bye. I watch as the guard takes him back through the vast labyrinth of concrete, steel, glass and bars, doors that shut with a kind of finality that we don't hear much in the outside world unless you are a fan of *Oz*.

Then we go to visit Jason Baldwin. He is heartbreakingly buoyant. The years in this place have not weighed down his spirit. I read him a poem that Damien had written about him, and the look on his face is priceless. He is grateful for the thousands of supporters that write to him from all over the world. He works in the law library, helping other inmates with their cases, and, through this service, he possesses a formidable knowledge of the legal system. I promise to write, and I encourage him to write his story, like a letter to the world.

And, finally, we visit Jessie Misskelley. He shows me the tattoo on top of his head, a clockface with Roman numerals. He plans to have the hands of the clock tattooed on with the exact time of his release, to commemorate it forever, when that time comes. He is adorable, and full of boundless hope. And he has the last thing that would be expected from someone serving life in prison: optimism. His outlook is impossibly sunny.

I wish our nation had as good a forecast. My friend Damien is sitting in prison for a crime he did not commit. And, in the face of resounding, exonerating evidence, the WM3 are still in prison. Could you imagine sitting in a cell for twelve years for something you didn't do? Our judicial system is quick when it comes to sentencing people to life and death, but it's unbearably slow when it needs to correct its own errors. Even if Damien, Jason and Jessie were freed today, they've still been wrongfully imprisoned for all this time. How much longer can we allow this injustice to go on?

conservatives like to procrastinate

Whenever I would witness some sort of injustice, I could understand it intellectually, and be angry about it in a very distant way, but knowing Damien Echols and his wife now as intimately as I do my feelings about the issues have changed dramatically. He wrote me the other day about the Elvis biopic on CBS. He wanted to know if I had seen it and what I thought. He said seeing it filled him with an unbearable longing to be back home. He was overcome with sorrow because he wanted to see Graceland again. All of us on the outside take Graceland for granted, and by Graceland I'm not just talking about fried peanut butter and banana sandwiches and dying from an overdose of prescription drugs while sitting on the toilet. Graceland is freedom, the right to make choices for yourself about where to go, what to do, how we will spend our weekends, our weekdays, our lives. It sickens me to know someone I love does not have this freedom, and misses it as badly and in more ways than I could ever imagine.

Perhaps the way we could abolish the death penalty is to do something much like the popular "Take Your Daughter to Work Day"—we could have a "Take Your Local Death Row Inmate to Work Day." Of course, there are a lot of horrifying people who are on death row, but if a close watch is kept on the worst ones the rest, the majority, are unlikely to kill again. When we are forced to personalize issues like the death penalty, actually put a face to a name, shake the hand of the accused, shoot the shit with those about to be shot, we cannot help but think again about what we are doing. It's likely that we might want to save their lives as well as our own.

We cannot lock people up and throw away the key. We cannot allow our courts to have the power over life and death. What if someone makes a mistake? It happens more than we realize. The justice system in this country is seriously flawed, and we should not wait until we are personally betrayed by it to take action.

Even those who are guilty deserve compassion. We are all human beings, and though there might be some of us who commit inhuman acts we have to remember that criminals are not born, they are made. Abuse begets abuse, and our society has too many built-in inequities and injustices and fuckovers that could make anyone on the shady side of it want to shoot up his or her workplace.

Most conservatives want to think that life is fair, since it is likely to have been more than fair to them. They like to ignore the heavy burden of inequality because they don't have to carry much of it.

Most conservatives also believe in the death penalty, but not abortion, which proves they like to procrastinate. Where do their arguments about the sanctity of life and how every child is a child of God go when it comes to taking the life of an alleged criminal? Why is life only sacred when it's convenient for them? It's the stupidity of us referring to those who bomb abortion clinics and murder doctors who terminate pregnancy "pro-lifers" that keeps them in gunpowder and homemade explosive devices. We need to call them "pro-deathers." The idiots who stand in front of clinics in order to harass young women walking in, bombarding them with gory, blown-up photographs of dismembered fetuses are often the same dummies screaming "Fry 'em!" in front of prisons during executions. It is clear that life is not as sacred as their own hypocrisy and ignorance, which they safeguard with a scary, steadfast devotion.

Watch how mad these angry, self-righteous dumbfucks get when you point out the inconsistencies in their beliefs. I love to aggravate them because even though they could tell me to go to hell, which would be far preferable than an Operation Rescue fund-raiser, I know their seething will only win them a lifetime of TMJ and high blood pressure. When you confront pissed-off people, try to piss them off even more. The rage you inspire in them will end up hurting them way more than it will ever hurt you, as long as you can avoid becoming totally infuriated yourself. The best tactic is to laugh at them.

Nothing brings their blood to a boil faster than a smug chuckle at their expense. Of course, then you may run the risk of them killing you, but perhaps if they get the death penalty for your murder they're likely to have a change of heart about capital punishment and even convert some of their ridiculous friends, so it might all be worth it in the end.

I am glad to know Damien Echols, and I am proud to be the publisher of his memoir, *Almost Home.* He tells his own remarkable story with grace and a sense of humor that seems impossible for someone in a situation like his. At my insistence, he has also submitted his work to numerous literary magazines and journals, and now has quite an interesting career as a writer, which brings him much personal satisfaction, introduces him to an entirely new world and gives him hope. He has the opportunity to speak his truth, making us all aware of the fragility of freedom, how it is easily lost, how it is not something to be taken lightly.

WHY I HAVE CHOSEN TO STAY AND FIGHT

"our revolution is long overdue."
—notorious c.h.o.

I **want to map out** an exit strategy for this book. Exit strategies are in demand, and even though George Bush yet still refuses to put a timetable on Iraq, we as a nation are fortunate in that we will be witness to an elaborate and stunningly dramatic exit for the Bush administration, if we are really lucky, and we can take our country back and try to clean up all the damage that has been done in the previous eight years.

I think that any proper exit strategy is to retreat into oneself, a turtle pulling back into its shell. Returning to Witch Mountain, or wherever you came from. To remove yourself from the situation so that you might recognize yourself again.

When I was a very young girl in San Francisco, the city had a terrible November. First, there was the Jonestown massacre, where over nine hundred men, women, children—black, white, Asian, Latino—were forced to commit ritual suicide by their leader, Jim Jones. This was certainly an exit strategy, and yet not the one that should have been implemented. The terrible deaths had occurred in Guyana, but the headquarters were still in San Francisco. Coincidentally, my grandparents were looking for a suitable venue for their fiftieth wedding anniversary party, and since the People's Temple members were not going to be needing the building my family snatched it up, pulling down police tape and replacing it with paper chains and streamers. My mom loves to party, and she hates to pay retail. But San Francisco barely noticed. It was in a state of shock. Over nine hundred of our people died, forced out to the jungle by a madman, with an exit strategy that was too permanent, too secretive, too insane, too ugly. The city mourned deeply as the rest of the world looked on in horror.

Then a disgruntled assemblyman assassinated Mayor Moscone and the highly popular and influential Harvey Milk, the first openly gay elected official. People were overwhelmed. Candlelight marches turned into riots. No one knew a way out of their grief and rage. My exit strategy then, as a little girl, was to vow that one day I would carry on in the tradition of Harvey Milk, that even though he had not survived his message would live on through me. I wasn't sure how that was going to happen, but it just kinda did. I exited grief and fear and my grandparents' golden anniversary and I entered womanhood and my warrior nature.

Now I want to flee from the new pope, Benedict XVI, whose first real statement as pope spoke out against *Harry Potter*. When there is a war on, a mysterious, terrifying, random, dangerous, apocalyptic situation, getting worse day by day, and, at the center of it, Iraq, from which all manner of evil seems to originate or is in rapid transit to, why is it suddenly important to take on a popular children's novel, a series of books that have brought excitement back to literacy and made reading cool once again. Reading is fundamental, as the old '70s saying goes. But religion goes off when it is fundamental. The Christian fundamentalists are exactly as closed-minded as the Islamic fundamentalists. If they could just see each other, if they could let their turbans and mullets and veils and Toni home perms down for a second, they would be able to see they have much in common, and much to offer each other. The exit strategy of the war on terrorism is a big potluck picnic, with fundamentalists from both sides participating in blueberry pie–eating contests, three-legged races, pin the tail on the infidel . . . getting down deep into the nature of who we are, and we can see the similarities are astounding, and that when I look at you I am looking in a mirror, a fun-house mirror but a mirror nonetheless.

When we can become really honest with ourselves, and deeply ponder what we want, where we want to go, what we want to do, we are at the perfect beginning, because we are, right at that moment, at the heart of who we are, and any action taken from that place is going to be a glorious one. Much of the writing in this book originated on my blog, and it represents many years of getting deeper into my own heart.

I found that making my thoughts heard online has brought me to an incredible community of other bloggers, who have taken me further into my own quest for truth than anyone could have imagined.

Bloggers have altered the way we view the news. Censorship and propaganda cannot go undetected in the blogosphere. Through the steady devotion of bloggers to tell the truth, to make their stories known, to communicate, to exist, loud and clear, we are blessed with an entirely new way to experience media. The news sources we relied on, the ones we feared would betray us with lies to protect their corporate allies, are no longer needed. We had a revolution in news, and it is all D-I-Y, grassroots, people working from their homes, stealing time on the job, to make sure America gets to stay beautiful and free and all that shit. Americablog.com, Dailykos.com, Atrios.blogspot.com and Buzzflash.com are just a few of the bloggers who are making a difference in the way America gets its news. Without freedom of information, we have no freedom. Without access to the truth, we are powerless. With mainstream media more under the control of government agencies, moving the terrorist alerts up and down like the mercury of a thermometer, gauging how liberal or conservative the country happens to be leaning, how can we really know what is happening? Fortunately, different individuals have been able to break through and allow themselves to be heard over the propaganda. The more the mainstream press ignores them, the more powerful they become.

Watching this new America unfold has made me truly welcome the emergence of the underground. I trust the bloggers more than the nightly news because even though everyone has an agenda, theirs are closer to mine. In these times, we must just try to get closer to ourselves, get back to who we are. Identifying ourselves in the unrelenting storm of false information is one way bloggers can help. Protecting the truth by becoming bloggers ourselves, instead of retreating into lies and twisted political posturing, needs to become our way of life. Choosing to stay and fight for ourselves is the only way we can survive.

updates to the paperback edition

WHO DO YOU THINK YOU ARE?

mapquest equality

I have to be very good-natured about all the racism and ignorance that I encounter because if I got angry at every single incident, I would wear myself out.

People ask me what it was like to make *Charlie's Angels*, and I have to force a smile and remind myself that they don't know better, and they are trying their best to be friendly. But it isn't funny to me, and it is starting to make me very depressed. It is not enough that there are so few Asian American women working in the entertainment industry. There has to be veiled and outright hostility toward the ones who are here.

But the countless interviewers and talk show hosts would never view their comments as hostile in the least. They cannot comprehend the fact that they might be racist, because they are so used to racism it feels like a second skin—one they can feel comfortable in because no one judges the color of it. No one would ever dream of mistaking

Mary J. Blige for Faith Evans, even in jest—especially in jest. Anyone who would infer that P. Diddy was actually Big Daddy Kane would be immediately fired, and likely banned from broadcasting forever and ever. Yet it somehow is totally okay to ask me why I left *The View*.

In remembering the remarkable life of Rosa Parks—and I am once again incredibly moved at the scope and power of the Civil Rights Movement—what I want to know is, how do we get there? If only it were possible to MapQuest equality. "When you get to democracy, turn LEFT."

Although racism still exists in a very real way for African Americans, white people have the sense to do it in private. It is not acceptable to be openly racist toward black people, but it still seems to be open season on the rest of us: Asians, Latinos, gays, lesbians—pretty much all other minorities. Learning the history of the Civil Rights Movement, committing to memory all the steps along the way, is the only thing I can think to do in trying to somehow re-create it today.

I was on a radio talk show where an African American woman called in to caution me about comparing the Civil Rights Movement to the fight for gay marriage, but it isn't like you can possibly conflate the two struggles. Injustice is injustice. It is that I wish to learn from example, for us to take the great strides made by African Americans in this country and use them like a map to take those remaining behind the lines of inequality to freedom.

translation for DUMMIES

People ask me why, since I myself am married to a man, would I work so hard to make gay marriage a reality? I answer that, today, no one questions the white students who went to Mississippi to march with Martin Luther King Jr. That sets them straight, as it were, pretty fast. Still, I don't understand why that isn't obvious. It feels like a dumb question to me.

Another dumb question I got on a radio talk show was, why I go for such easy targets like the Bush administration. Is it that I am too scared to take on a real enemy like Islam? I just answered, Islam is not my enemy. I am not oppressed by Islam. Of course, oppression exists in the fundamentalist movements there, but Christian fundamentalists here are the ones who get me down. Why these people want to start fights with me, I will never know. Is it because of my race? That they are so desperately racist, that whenever they see someone who is not Bill Bennett talking about what is wrong with this country, it makes them go crazy?

I imagine it is the combination of my gender and my connection to the queer community, as well as my Asian features, that makes some conservatives want to blow up with straight-white-male entitlement and rage. Since my purpose is not to explain my race, as often Asian characters on TV shows or in movies are there to do, most don't know what to make of me.

I wish someone would explain straight-white-male entitlement to me. Why do I, with as much right to be here as anyone, have to constantly translate their confusion and double-speak? Why must I constantly try to accommodate their racist, sexist, homophobic views, just because they are trying to understand me?

GIVE PEACE A CHANCE

The terrible Iraq war continues, for three years now, and Bush won't bring the troops home. Isn't that typical of a straight man—unable to prematurely withdraw?

I performed at "Bring 'Em Home Now!"—the massive antiwar concert at the Hammerstein Ballroom last night, and it was a lavish, star-studded, sold-out affair. I saw lots of people I love, like Alan Cumming, who wasn't performing, just looking gorgeous; Peaches, who rocked the house and was incredibly sexy and awe-inspiring (and name checked me!); the great Rufus Wainwright (who is sooooo fine, this woman I was sitting next to swooned, "He will never love me." I said, "He might. Maybe not in the way you are thinking of though . . . alas . . . we need a refuge from all this beauty . . ."); Fischerspooner; Steve Earle; Moby with Laura Dawn; Bright Eyes; Chuck D; Michael Stipe—all kinds of rock elite, proving that if the politicians can't be bothered to save us, music surely will.

I did a set, then walked out into the audience to find my friends. I didn't manage to see them, but I met a couple of guys from Iraq Veterans Against the War, Geoffrey Millard and Jose Vasquez. Geoffrey told me that he watched my DVDs while he was over there to keep his spirits up, which just blew my mind. They are courageous and deeply passionate about peace, having seen war firsthand, and their work is vital to seeing an end to this madness. Everyone should check them out!

I sat in an overflowing box on the side and watched Cindy Sheehan, who brought the crowd to tears and fury. Through her activism, she has really helped turn this nation around, because she was brave and angry enough to question Bush, and we all share her frustration and grief over her son Casey. It makes me so mad, all this death and destruction, and for what? It is still happening because the government cannot and will not admit that they were wrong. They cannot admit they were lying. We must hold them accountable. My enthusiasm and commitment to doing whatever I can to help end the war were renewed again and again. I am honored to have been able to participate at such a historic and powerfully moving event, and I hope that its impact will be felt around the world.

RACE IN AMERICA

What I'm hearing, which is sort of scary, is they all want to stay in Texas. Everyone is so overwhelmed by the hospitality. And so many of the people in the arena here, you know, were underprivileged anyway, so this—this [she chuckles slightly] is working very well for them."

Eew. This is what Barbara Bush said about the Hurricane Katrina refugees at the Astrodome in Houston. The worst thing is that she actually went and visited them. Haven't they suffered enough? I think it is just disgusting. Her attitude is like, "Poverty is adorable! Look at all these cute, cute, cute poor people! They should be thankful for Katrina because if it weren't for the flood they wouldn't be able to enjoy this nice, nice stadium! They're much better off aren't they? I ♥ the lower class!"

It just clearly shows that she has no understanding of what happened, if she actually thinks that being poor somehow makes the disaster less of one, because now instead of a small, cramped, and overcrowded apartment, they get a huge, cramped, and overcrowded stadium. What is she saying? "Oh they didn't have anything to lose, so what does it matter if they lost it all?" If this is what they think of the poor, then what do they think of the rest of America? What is thought about the soldiers who were killed in Iraq? "Oh they were so young, they were barely alive anyway. No one notices they're gone anyway! It's working well for them!"

I never had any soft feelings for Barbara Bush. She looks like a grandma and a grandpa at the same time, which would normally make me like her, but for some reason, her politics make her Quaker Oats appearance unappealing. She's like hot breakfast cereal sprinkled with broken glass and fake compassion. She is like a multigrain muffin with cranberries and thumbtacks. She is the former first lady and the current worst lady. And she is not working well for me.

I am very sad for New Orleans, and for all the communities destroyed by the hurricane. But New Orleans in particular is a painful loss because the city is very special to me. The news coverage was extensive and predictably racist. When black people steal, it's looting. When white people steal, it's because emergency workers are slow to act and they must feed their families.

I have spent a good deal of time in New Orleans, particularly in the stylish and historic French Quarter. It's amazing to look at, of course, with the wrought-iron balconies, the candy heart–colored houses that line the street, the tangle of vine and trellis everywhere. To call it haunted would be an understatement. Every dark street and alley holds its own moldy secret. The mythology of the town, steeped in the spiritual legacy of slavery and hundreds of years of racial unrest, add to its chaotic charm. The sweet smell of decay blowing up from the river across Charles Street always symbolized the decadence of New Orleans, like rotting magnolias, putrefying in the rigor-mortis grasp of a dead debutante. Beautiful and horrible. At once sacred and profane, and likely the only place in America that can be described as such.

The city is fickle as the heart of a Southern belle. It will welcome you with open arms, girls gone wild, and fair weather; then it will mug you, blow all your windows in, and make you throw up Mardi Gras beads. I have always been lucky; the city likes me, as far as I can tell, but that was due to my own efforts. I've spent late nights knocking three times at the door of Marie Laveau's crypt, carefully carving my initials in the dusty cemetery rock, asking permission to live on the quiet end of Bourbon Street. I never did find a place to live there, but I always thought I still might, until now.

I saw a lost and fearful-looking Doberman on a rooftop, and I wished I had a giant ark, and I could sail down into the city and save him. Then I would pick up all the other animals and people that needed help, two by two. Two trannies here, two hookers there. A pair of wet and miserable Goths with black Manic Panic hair dye running into their red, unbelieving eyes. I want to save them all.

The rest of the country is finally waking up to something that many of us have known for a long time. The Bush administration does not care about poor people or black people. It is evident in its flagrant disregard for these communities ravaged by the hurricane. The delayed response for emergency services clearly shows how little our government cares, and how little our government is willing to do for us—unless they are trying to cover up for their own faulty decision-making. I am glad they have finally fucked it up so badly they can't begin to recover from it no matter how many times Bush flies over the Gulf Coast, but it unfortunately had to impact those who least deserved it. The poor were not responsible for Bush being in office, but they are the ones who had to pay the ultimate price for it. The media is trying to cover for themselves too. The racism in our nation has flooded our collective consciousness, and the horrors that lie underneath these waters are far more grisly than anything that will be found in Katrina's wake.

r.i.p., richard pryor

When I was little, all I ever wanted to be was Richard Pryor. I knew it was impossible to grow up and be him, since he was already him, and was doing very well as himself. Still, I did grow up, and bent and shaped my life according to his. As a performer, I always think of him when I am onstage, sweating like crazy under the hot lights. I will never be as good as he was, or as important, but I will always be a tribute, and I will always pay homage. I am struck dumb with sadness at the news of his death, and my sympathy goes out to his family and friends, and all the fans out there like me, who loved him like I do.

FEMINISM IS A FEMINIST ISSUE

I love the new Dove ads with the curvy girls in their underwear. They are hot. I was kind of shocked by them at first, mostly because we never, ever see any images of real-looking women in the media, much less unclothed. The way we see "normal" in advertising, movies, and TV is completely abnormal. The thin yet muscular bodies we are used to seeing up there are actually quite rare down here. In real life, few people are like that. Isn't it weird that we never use ourselves to sell something to ourselves? That authenticity is a shocking new marketing campaign and not the norm? I think the women in the Dove ads look great. They look sexy and healthy and beautiful, and that they are not "models" is wrong, because they should be modeling everything!

Whenever I see an ad with lots of painfully thin girls in it, I am usually turned off to the product. I feel like it must not be for me. It probably wouldn't matter but this happens thousands of times a day. Pretty soon, I suspect the entire world is not for me. It must only be for the thinner, richer, whiter, and younger crowd. You start to believe nobody cares about you, that even your money isn't good enough for them. I love that Dove is not too good for my money, and its inclusive advertising makes me want to buy its product.

I hope other companies wake up. Clothes do not look better on thinner people. They just look like clothes I am not supposed to wear and therefore will not be purchasing. Everybody knows that. It is not like anyone looks at a model wearing something and immediately thinks that it will look the same on them. Self-consciousness is just as strong an instinct as wanting to "buy in to" the glamorous life. I can't understand why advertisers still don't get this. Besides, I want to see more sexy women in their underwear.

stress signal in south dakota

South Dakota just passed legislation that will make nearly all abortions illegal, and the state and the anti-choice groups are hoping to ride this all the way to the Supreme Court. This is appalling and unbelievable, and this is happening in America. We are losing the sense of who we are. We are losing our freedoms daily, one by one, like fingers from a leprous hand. Our once cherished beliefs like democracy and independence are decaying and dropping off to reveal a withered stump of a nation.

We can't go out like this.

FAMILY VALUES

I was listening to a debate on banning gay and lesbian adoptions last night on the radio, which made me so furious, even more mad than the ever-present, early-evening LA traffic in front of me. There are so many children in the world who need parents, and these people are trying to keep them from finding homes, because of their own need to somehow demonize homosexuality and define it like it is some kind of inherent weakness. It makes me sick and it makes me want to be in a mosh pit with them so I can throw an elbow into their faces.

What exactly do these homophobic idiots think is good for children? For them to just waste away unwanted and unloved in the system because at least they won't be exposed to Project Runway? The Dinah Shore Golf Tournament? I happen to think that gays and lesbians would be better at taking care of children, because the truth is, it is hard to be different in this society, no matter what is said about tolerance, or how many new holidays are created, and when you have to struggle because you are not like the rest, you just tend to be better than the rest. They try to reason that the breakup rate is high for homosexual couples, but when every other heterosexual marriage ends in divorce, isn't that the pot calling the kettle "noncommittal"?

thank you, ang lee

Congratulations on winning the Oscar for Best Director. I loved the film *Brokeback Mountain.* I sat in the theater and cried so much, because you told the story with such dignity and truth. I have been working in the gay and lesbian community for over twenty years, as an activist and artist, and your film did more to humanize our struggle than anything else so far in our history.

Thank you for your courage and your magnificent artistry. You make me proud that an Asian person can accomplish so much in this very racist and homophobic industry. To me you make an impossible dream a reality. I hope to one day make such great strides as you. You are an inspiration to everyone, for not only are you an incredible filmmaker, you take on such intensely controversial political issues, and challenge the conservatives with the simple, beautiful art of storytelling. Where they have given us hate and fear, you have shown us the glory of love and the undeniable power of the human heart. Thank you for all of your films and especially thank you for *Brokeback Mountain.*

Best,

Margaret Cho

WHAT WOULD BOWIE DO?

pat robertson

Pat Robertson said we should just assassinate Venezuela's President Chavez, calling him a "dangerous enemy" for his leftist views and because he controls enough oil to make Robertson think he could hurt America. I am not sure exactly how we can be hurt by oil, other than the possibility that it would raise our cholesterol levels sky-high, but Robertson thinks so, and he is hoppin' mad.

It is nice when our religious leaders talk like terrorists. The sad part is I know that lots of Americans would not see this comment as inappropriate or out of line. We have reached a terrible era in this country of unbridled stupidity. It is a war between the haves and the have-nots, but we aren't talking about money. This time it is about intelligence.

Robertson said it would be cheaper to just assassinate Chavez instead of going to war with him. A penny saved is a Venezuelan president assassinated. I guess that is the trouble with war. It's expensive.

Never mind the incredible loss of life and crimes against humanity. Pricey! Plus it is rich coming from the 700 Club, which should now call itself the 187 Club, because its members are supposed to live by the motto, "What would Jesus do?" Something makes me think Jesus wouldn't do that. But this is not your father's Christianity. Today, we have kick-ass Christians, who shoot first and turn the other cheek later.

Robertson finally apologized for saying that the U.S. should assassinate Venezuelan President Chavez. At first, he tried to deny ever saying it and blamed the media for taking his remarks out of context. Then he just hunkered down and said he was sorry.

I think what happened is the CIA was about to assassinate Chavez and then Pat Robertson fucked up its whole plan. Now, due to the controversy everyone would be watching and any attempt would be too suspicious.

Pat Robertson always says the most crazy shit. He said that because of Gay Days at Disney World, a meteor would hit Florida. I don't think that is possible. If any meteor were to hit Florida because of rampant gayness, it would have to be Key West, not Disney World. He also claimed that feminism caused women to kill their children, practice witchcraft, and become lesbians. He's not smart, but he is sorry.

THE RIGHT TO LIFE

I don't know why it surprises me that they executed Tookie, but somehow I thought that this was all an elaborate staging for a last-minute reprieve. It seemed impossible that they would put him to death, with so much public protest, with so much to say in his defense. If they can kill him, they can kill us all, without reason, without mercy.

"The state of California may have extinguished the life of Stanley Tookie Williams, but they have not managed to extinguish the hope for a better world." —Angela Davis

RESOURCE GUIDE

American Civil Liberties Union (ACLU): *http://www.aclu.com*

Asian American Legal Defense and Education Fund: *http://www.aaldef.org*

Asian Equality: *http://www.asianequality.org*

Best Friends: *http://www.bestfriends.org*

Code Pink: *http://www.codepink4peace.org*

Equality Federation: *http://www.federationlgbt.org*

Feminist Majority Foundation: *http://www.feminist.org*

Freedom to Marry: *http://www.freedomtomarry.org*

Free the West Memphis Three: *http://www.wm3.org*

Gay and Lesbian Alliance Against Defamation (GLAAD):
   http://www.glaad.org

Human Rights Campaign (HRC): *http://www.hrc.org*

Humane Society: *http://www.hsus.org*

Immigration Equality: *http://www.immigrationequality.org*

Iraq Veterans Against the War: *http://www.ivaw.net*

Lambda Legal: *http://www.lambdalegal.org*

Marriage Equality USA: *http://www.marriageequality.org*

MoveOn: *http://www.moveon.org*

NAACP: *http://www.naacp.org*

NARAL Pro-Choice America: *http://www.naral.org*

National AIDS Fund: *http://www.aidsfund.org*

National Black Justice Coalition: *http://www.nbjcoalition.org*

National Center for Lesbian Rights: *http://www.nclrights.org*

National Center for Transgender Equality: *http://www.nctequality.org*

National Gay and Lesbian Task Force (NGLTF):

   http://www.thetaskforce.org

National Organization for Women (NOW): *http://www.now.org*

Partners Task Force for Gay and Lesbian Couples: *http://buddybuddy.com*

Parents, Families, and Friends of Lesbians and Gays (PFLAG):

   http://www.pflag.org

Planned Parenthood: *http://www.plannedparenthood.com*

Rainbow World Fund: *http://www.rainbowfund.org*

Servicemembers Legal Defense Network: *http://www.sldn.org*

Tookie's Corner: *http://www.tookie.com*

Veterans for Peace: *http://www.veteransforpeace.org*

ACKNOWLEDGMENTS

Great thanks to Sean McDonald and to Julie Grau, for bravely publishing this book.

Thanks to David Vigliano, rock star literary agent.

Thanks to Ava Stander, my sister and true thug family.

Thanks to Damien Echols and Lorri Davis, for sharing their love with me. Love love love!

Thanks to Keri Smith, my assistant, but more like my friendly neighborhood genius.

Thanks to Bruce Daniels, for that time he made that spaghetti and when he did the only known listless handjob ever captured on film.

Thanks to Lorene Machado, for being such a great director and also for sending me countless pictures of Handsome Hank, my favorite pit bull.

Thanks to Austin Young, for the fabulous cover! Thanks to Patty Hearst, for fashion inspiration.

Thanks to Princess Farhana of Hollywood, for teaching me figure eights with a sit.

Thanks to: Mark at Buzzflash.com; Markos at Dailykos.com; Duncan at Atrios.blogspot.com; John and Joe at Americablog.com; Gene at Americanpoliticsjournal.com; Democraticunderground.com; and all the bloggers I've loved before.

Most of all, thanks to Al Ridenour, my husband, and the best friend I have ever had. You make me so very happy, habibi.